IN THE PRESENCE OF ENGLISH: MEDIA AND EUROPEAN YOUTH

IN THE PRESENCE OF ENGLISH: MEDIA AND EUROPEAN YOUTH

Editors

MARGIE BERNS
Purdue University/USA

KEES DE BOT
University of Groningen/The Netherlands

UWE HASEBRINK
University of Hamburg/Germany

 Springer

Margie Berns
Purdue University/USA

Kees de Bot
University of Groningen/The Netherlands

Uwe Hasebrink
University of Hamburg/Germany

Library of Congress Control Number:2006931702

ISBN -13: 978-0387-36893-1
ISBN -10: 0-387-36893-0

e-ISBN-13: 978-0387-36894-8
e-ISBN-10: 0-387-36894-9

Printed on acid-free paper.

9 8 7 6 5 4 3 2 1

springer.com

DEDICATION

To the memory of
Hans-Eberhard Piepho
February 15, 1929 – September 11, 2004

Contents

List of figures ix

List of tables xi

List of contributors xv

Preface xvii

Chapter 1   The presence of English: Sociocultural,
acquisitional, and media dimensions –
Margie Berns 1

Chapter 2   English in Europe – Margie Berns,
Marie-Thérèse Claes, Kees de Bot, Riet Evers,
Uwe Hasebrink, Ineke Huibregtse, Claude Truchot,
and Per van de Wijst 15

Chapter 3   An empirical approach to the presence of English –
Margie Berns 43

Chapter 4   Descriptive findings on the presence of English –
Kees de Bot, Riet Evers, and Ineke Huibregtse 53

Chapter 5   Determinants of contact, proficiency and attitudes –
Kees de Bot and Riet Evers 71

Chapter 6   English, youth and media environments –
Uwe Hasebrink 89

Chapter 7   In the presence of English: A resume after step
one of an international study – Uwe Hasebrink,
Margie Berns, and Kees de Bot 111

References 121

Appendix 137

Index 155

Figures

5.1   Main variables and indicators

5.2   Mixed model

Tables

3.1   Number of subjects from each school type - Belgium

3.2   Number of subjects from each school type - France

3.3   Number of subjects from each school type - Germany

3.4   Number of subjects from each school type - Netherlands

3.5   Country of birth by research group in percentages of the number of students from whom data are available (N)

4.1   Highest level of education of either parent by research group in percentages of the number of students from whom data are available (N)

4.2   Languages spoken at home by students in percentages of the number of students from whom data are available (N)

4.3   Estimated levels of language proficiency of parents and siblings, with the mean, the standard deviation (s.d.) and the number of students on which the means are based (N)

4.4   Contact with English by research group, with the mean (m), the standard deviation (s.d.) and the number of students on which the means are based (N)

4.5   Reported duration of listening to music in hours per week, with the mean, the standard deviation (s.d.) and the number of students who answered the question (N)

4.6   The language of the lyrics the students listen to and the importance they attach to the lyrics in percentages of the number of students per research group who answered the question (N)

4.7   Contact with English through watching TV and listening to radio: number of students answering "yes" in percentages of the total number of students per research group from whom data are available (N)

4.8   Frequency of watching English language TV programs and types of networks watched by research group in percentages of the number of students from whom data are available (N)

4.9   Contact with English during holidays by research group: number of students answering "yes" in percentage of the total number of students from whom data are available (N)

4.10   Classes of countries visited on holiday by research group in percentages of the number of students from whom data are available (N)

4.11   Likeability and importance of English as reported by the students with the mean, the standard deviation (s.d.) and the number of students who answered the question (N)

4.12   Opinions of the students on advantages of knowing English with the mean (m), the standard deviation (s.d.) and the number of students on which the means are based (N)

4.13   Self assessment for speaking, listening, writing and reading with the mean (m), the standard deviation (s.d.) and the number of students who answered the question (N)

4.14   Scores on the EFL Vocabulary Test with the mean, the standard deviation (s.d.) and the number of students who completed the test (N)

4.15   Acquisition of the English language: portions in percent attributed by the students to school media and other sources, with the mean, the standard deviation (s.d.) and the number of students from whom data are available (N)

5.1   Results analyses of variance

5.2   Results for main variables in groups

5.3   Proficiency scores in percentages

5.4   Family variables, contact, and proficiency. Direct and total effects: standardized estimates for total sample (N=1570)

5.5   Multi-sample analysis: unstandardized estimates of total effects

6.1   Dimensions of contact opportunities with the English language (factor analyses for all sub-samples and for the total sample; factor loadings)

6.2   Contacts with English and other characteristics of sub-groups with different media environments

6.3   Coping with different kinds of situations in sub-groups with different media environments

6.4   Importance of song lyrics in English and in national languages

6.5   Liking of languages and countries in groups with different patterns of attitudes to song lyrics (results for German sample only)

6.6   Liking and proficiency of English in groups with different patterns of attitudes to song lyrics

List of contributors

Margie Berns
Department of English
Purdue University
West Lafayette, Indiana
USA
berns@purdue.edu

Marie-Thérèse Claes
Faculty of Business
Asian University
Banglamung, Chonburi Thailand
mtclaes@asianust.ac.th

Kees de Bot
Department of Language and
Communication
University of Groningen
Groningen
The Netherlands
c.l.j.de.bot@let.rug.nl

Riet Evers
Dept. of Applied Linguistics
University of Nijmegen
The Netherlands
R.Evers@let.kun.nl

Uwe Hasebrink
Hans-Bredow-Institute for Media
Research
Hamburg
Germany
U.Hasebrink@hans-bredow-
institut.de

Ineke Huibregtse
IVLOS, Utrecht University
Utrecht
The Netherlands
I.Huibregtse@ivlos.uu.nl

Claude Truchot
GEPE
Université Marc Bloch
Strasbourg, France
Claude.Truchot@umb.u-strasbg.fr

Per van de Wijst
Faculty of Arts
Discourse Studies
Tilburg
The Netherlands
Per.vanderWijst@uvt.nl

Preface

In the Presence of English: Media and European Youth is the realization of a project first conceived in 1991 in Hamburg, Germany where Uwe Hasebrink, Ewart Skinner, and Margie Berns, with their respective specializations in media studies, international communication, and world Englishes, met and discovered intersecting interests. In that meeting they sketched out plans for a questionnaire survey to be distributed in Hamburg schools that would investigate secondary school pupils access to and use of media, their access to and use of English, and their attitudes concerning these and related topics. A year later several hundred young people in selected schools completed the questionnaire. The findings from this initial investigation appeared in a book chapter by Hasebrink, Berns, and Skinner (1997) and were reported on at conferences in North America and Europe.

Eventually Kees de Bot (The Netherlands) was inspired to join Berns and Hasebrink (Ewart Skinner had moved on to other projects). Eventually we decided to extend and refine the project by building upon its interdisciplinary and international potential. From this point on the study gained increasing momentum and scope and individual team members contributed variously to what became a major undertaking. The size and complexity of the project made it not only time intensive, but time extensive as well. With limited sources of financial support, progress was slow, at times arduous, and the gap between data collection and finished manuscript was greater than anticipated.

Distribution of labor among us kept the task manageable. Kees recruited additional researchers in Belgium and the Netherlands; Margie recruited from France; and Uwe extended the survey in Germany. Team member expertise now included business communication, psycholinguistics, and foreign language teaching. Together the expanded group, now numbering eight, refined the design of the expanded study that came to include more schools and school types in more diverse linguistic, social, and cultural contexts within Belgium, France, Germany, and the Netherlands. Kees also enlisted the assistance of Riet Evers, who managed the data and the analyses as well as the design and the production of the tables. Margie took on the overall coordination of the project from drafting of chapters by team members through the manuscript production. The three of us shared in the editing process.

The book you now hold in your hands is the outcome of this effort. With its completion, we hope one day to conduct similar investigations in a wider range of countries. With the identification of researchers and scholars in each location, future phases can commence for surveys in two regional clusters, namely, Italy, Portugal, and Spain, and Uzbekistan, Hungary, and

Russia. Ideally, we would like to gather additional data at a wider variety of sites elsewhere in Belgium, France, Germany, and the Netherlands.

And if the team is granted a long life and a generous supply of resources, it would welcome the opportunity to conduct a longitudinal study in the same four countries included in the present study. With this data, we could document changes in the presence of English over time in the lives of young people in Europe.

The accomplishment this book represents is due to the invaluable, incalculable time and energy, foresight and insight, good humor and patience, and knowledge and skill of the Marie-Thérèse Claes, Riet Evers, Ineke Huibregtse, Claude Truchot, and Per van de Wijst. Translating survey instruments, collecting data, writing and co-writing chapters, adapting procedures, and hosting team meetings are just a sampling of their substantial contributions. For scrupulous attention to each aspect of the statistical side of the project, Riet Evers merits additional recognition; our appreciation of her advanced knowledge of and experience with LISREL analysis cannot be overstated.

It is said that the devil is in the details. Fortunately, we were able to rely on a fearless few to keep him at bay. For this we gratefully acknowledge Claudia Lampert, researcher at the Hans Bredow Institute, for organizing data collection in Germany, Christèle Agraz for data collection in France, and Nicole Livengood, Lucie Moussu, Gigi Taylor, and Yufeng Zhang, research assistants at Purdue University, for background data and manuscript editing, and, last but not least, Julie Taylor, ESL Program secretary at Purdue University, for word processing and formatting of text and tables.

Margie Berns, Purdue University
Kees de Bot, Universiteit Groningen
Uwe Hasebrink, Universität Hamburg/
Hans-Bredow Institut

Chapter 1

THE PRESENCE OF ENGLISH SOCIOCULTURAL, ACQUISITIONAL, AND MEDIA DIMENSIONS

Margie Berns

1.1   INTRODUCTION

In contemporary Europe, issues of language have taken on new urgency and importance. Two developments have contributed to current debates and discussions on linguistic matters. One is globalization of the world's economy and the accompanying increase in the spread of English. The other is the institutionalization of the 25-member European Union (EU); with its increasing multilingualism and multiculturalism as more countries gain entry over the coming years.   The 2005 enlargement added 10 Southern and Central European countries, which increased the multilingual and multicultural dimensions of Europe; the number of official EU languages also expanded to 21, and Polish, Hungarian, and Latvian now need to be accommodated within EU institutions and incorporated into practices and policies of every Member State.   In 2007 the diversity broadens even further with the 2007 membership of Bulgaria and Romania and the addition of Irish as an EU official language.   Expansion heightens the necessity for EU citizens to have not only knowledge and understanding of one another, but also a means of making this understanding possible.   Against this background the value of knowing a foreign language is evident. English for many of the Europeans, especially young people, is that very language.

Contemporary European youth live in a world in which globalism and localism seem to be in competition, in which information access and cultural transformations are increasingly driven by media and technology, and in which the uses of English in daily life are expanding and the demand for instruction is increasing.   These linguistic and cultural realities are the background and impetus for our study of the intersection of English, media, and youth in Europe. These elements in conjunction merit closer consideration, in our view, in light of explicit policies and programs supported by various agencies within and associated with the European Union to foster cross-cultural communication, strengthen a sense of unity among the EU's 456,863 million citizens (European Commission, 2005) and protect the multilingual and multicultural quality of Europe.

1.1.1   English

English plays a special role in the European context because it is the most frequently used language of communication in interactions between two Europeans or a European and another speaker of English – whether a native or non-native speaker – from anywhere in the world.   Among Europeans, it is considered to be the most useful language to know apart from the mother tongue. Outside of work or school, English also serves as a means of interpersonal communication for Europeans taking part in a variety of activities, for example, sporting events, school visits and exchanges, or family outings and vacations. English also serves as a means of interpersonal communication between Europeans who have no other language in common when they participate in email exchanges or internet chat rooms. According to a 2006 EU Commission study, more than half (51%) of 450 million citizens of the EU can understand one another in English (European Commission, 2006, p.4).

English (as well as other languages) is used for cross-cultural communication through various programs, many of which are aimed at youth and supported by the European Commission's Directorate General for Education and Culture. One is a voluntary service scheme that provides structured cooperation between youth organizations, local authorities, and project leaders. Primarily, it provides young people with opportunities for mobility and informal learning. Activities associated with town twinning and sporting events, for example, bring young people from different cultures and languages together.   Such contacts become vehicles for the establishment of networks requiring communication between people regardless of particular interest in or knowledge of respective languages and cultures. The surge in opportunities for communication has not only has increased contact with and motivations for using English; it has lead to more young people across Europe knowing English with a higher level of proficiency than was the case in previous generations.

The desirability of the extent of the presence of English in Europe is debated. There are the pragmatists who advocate - and have done so for a long while - getting on with accepting that English is not going to go away in the foreseeable future and who urge adopting social and educational policies that ensure access to its learning and competent use (see, e.g., Ammon, 1994; Cenoz & Jessner, 2000; Gnutzmann, 1999; Truchot, 1997;

see also Piepho, 1988, for a pedagogical perspective). The more idealistic see English as a significant threat to Europe's multilingual and multicultural diversity and champion efforts to restrict its learning and use (see, e.g., Pennycook, 1994; Phillipson, 1992; Skutnabb-Kangas, 2000).

1.1.2 Youth

Young people of the European Union between the ages of 15 and 24 make up nearly 13% of the population. These young people expect a lot from Europe, even while realizing it is their job to build it (European-Commission, 2001b). An EU study of languages clearly showed that the young are more linguistically able than their parents' generation.

Young people's role as leaders of change is relevant on this point. As they acquire new social networks and identities and feel the requirements for appropriate language styles, some of which they will keep and some of which they will discard, they perpetuate the status quo, change it, and/or lead it. The teenage years are sensitive ones for adult identity development and are a period where language shift occurs, establishing patterns of use for later years. Youth adopt, adapt, and reject values and styles in not only choices of pastimes or dress but also in languages and how they are used. Among youth as consumers and exploiters of media products, the issues of media contact and use, language and identity, and cultural formation come together.

1.1.3 Media

The areas of English language and media are closely interwoven. The global distribution of American popular culture through film, television, and music with English as a medium illustrates the close connection between the areas of English language and media. Audiovisual media play a fundamental role in the development and transmission of social values and in the transmission, development and even construction of cultural identities. The presence of English language media, especially from the United States and its dominant place in the lives of European youth, raise questions about their social and cultural identity (Hasebrink, 2001). Does contact with and exposure to English and American culture change the culture of those who avail themselves of such media products as films, television programming, music, radio broadcasts and computer interactions in which English is the language of communication and expression?

The use of newer technologies also is integral in young people's lives (d'Haenens, 2001). Among the 15-25 year old age group, as reported in Eurobarometer 55 (European Commission, 2001b), the percentage of those who regularly go online, use a computer, and play video games has more than doubled since 1997. Regular mobile phone users in this same age bracket number 80%. Another indicator of the relationship between youth and computer use is the fact that the rate of internet penetration depends upon the rate at which families of 15-year-olds acquire home computers (Eurydice, 2004). (For data on the nature and extent of changes in access to and use of these internet tools with accession of new member states, see European Commission, 2003).

This interdisciplinary research project was informed by studies in media and communication, sociolinguistics, social psychology, and second language acquisition. Each area provides concepts and perspectives to structure the investigation on issues and topics we considered key: the world Englishes paradigm, language and cultural identity, socio-cultural theory, input, multilingual acquisition, communicative competence, and cultivation theory.

1.2   SOCIOLINGUISTIC AND SOCIOCULTURAL CONSIDERATIONS

Since our specific interest in English was primarily its use rather than its formal properties, critical resources were studies of language in use, that is, how language functions in performing social roles and in structuring the identities of individuals and the culture of entire communities and societies.

1.2.1   World Englishes and cultural identity

The relatively new paradigm of world Englishes (WE) research contributed a sociolinguistic perspective on the diffusion and use of English in the global context (see Kachru, 1997, for an overview). A central feature of this approach is the distinction between uses of English for international and for intranational purposes and the concomitant recognition that, for example, an East Asia's requirements for international comprehensibility are not the same as a South India's need for English to serve their own internal purposes. This distinction is captured in a model of three concentric circles (inner, outer, expanding), each representing a separate historical and social context of English spread (see Kachru, 1985). Europe is generally identified with the expanding (the outermost) circle because there English is used as the primary foreign language, and the number of its uses and users are increasing (see Berns, 1995b, for issues related to such identification).

Along with the formal characteristics of language acculturation, uses, or functions, are considered an equally important feature in understanding English in any context. Formal phonological, morphological, lexical, and semantic variation and functional allocation within domains and across society together constitute each variety of English and thus permit the recognition of varieties of English other than British or American, identified as inner circle varieties in Kachru's model. European English is one example of language acculturation, a product of what Ammon calls "the non-native speakers' right to linguistic peculiarities" (1998; 2000) (for more on European English, see also Carstensen, 1980; Denison, 1981; and Seidlhofer, 2001).

We take from the world Englishes paradigm the acceptance of multiple Englishes, regardless of which circle they develop within, because it de-emphasizes the native vs. non-native dichotomy and stresses identifying all who know and use it as speakers of English, independent of their level of proficiency or the extent of their use (see McArthur, 1998). This element informed our determination of who can and cannot be considered a user of English and our position that questions of proficiency and user status need to be considered as dependent upon the social and linguistic setting and contexts of the situation in which the learning and use of English take place.

As a global *lingua franca*, English functions as a means of communication between and among speakers of different languages - none of whom have English as their first language - in various settings around the world. This use of English contrasts with *international language*, which refers to its role in communication involving first as well as second-language English speakers. English serves Europeans use in both roles. It functions as the primary lingua franca of Europe, and growing numbers of Europeans use it in international communication within and beyond the region. A defining property of these roles for English is the negation of its narrow coupling with the worldviews of British or American culture, that is, English is "culturally neutral". The linguistic and sociolinguistic norms of inner circle speakers are no longer the arbiters of "correct" and "appropriate" use.

This separation of language and culture is essential in constructing – or deconstructing – European identity. Two particular perspectives interested us. One is the belief that the diffusion of English language elements – both formal and functional – into a language automatically leads to a penetration of the values of the respective culture and subsequently to the endangerment of this culture. Loss of cultural identity would ensue with worldwide cultural "McDonaldization".

Another view, additive rather than subtractive in nature, considers contact with and use of English as a means to an additional identity. The additive orientation is represented in cultural theory, most notably in the work of Geert Hofstede (1980, 1996), whose model of cross-cultural differences has become dominant. Rather than regard processes of acculturation and nativization as leading to uniformity when local traditions, values and social contexts meet, cultural theorists explore its effect of creating new hybrid forms of culture, language, and political organizations. Essential to this argument is Hofstede's (1996) interpretation of culture, which he describes as an all encompassing influence on the patterns of thinking, feeling and acting that every person has acquired in childhood and carries along through life (*mental programs*, in his terms). All who have gone through this learning process share these patterns and those belonging, say, to a national group, have patterns that give them a national identity, or culture. This identity has two aspects. The first consists of symbols, heroes, and rituals, and the second of values. The latter is of particular interest to our study because values affect attitudes – both toward a language, its roles and status, and toward its speakers and their culture.

It is these cultural values which are the more resilient to change and continue to show strong nation-state components, which Hofstede illustrates with three European cases. First, 2,000 years of history have not eliminated the difference in mentality between peoples once under Rome and those whose ancestors remained barbarians. Second, 400 years of neighborhood have not unified the mental programs of Dutch speakers on either side of the river separating the northern and southern part of the Low Countries. Third, 90 years of Swedish-Norwegian Union have not dissolved the difference between Swedes and Norwegians.

The learning of languages and multilingual acquisition are relevant in this regard when considering questions of identity loss because of the effects of globalization and the potential of English to replace local languages. Byram (1996, p.12) presents one point of view on the question of English as a European lingua franca that fits our perspective. He says, "if and when English becomes a European lingua franca it will embody and reflect a pan-European cultural identity, and be an additional identity, not one which replaces national identity" (see also Berns, 1995b).

1.3   SECOND LANGUAGE ACQUISITION SOCIAL ORIENTATION

Social orientations of both sociolinguistics and social psychology are complemented by theories of second language acquisition (SLA) research that view language in social more than psychological terms. Up until fairly recently, SLA researchers, following Chomsky, have restricted their interest to those aspects of language the learner needs to "master", with primary focus on syntax and morphology. In regarding second language acquisition as the subconscious or conscious processes by which a language other than the first language is learned in a natural or tutored setting, their study of the phenomenon is directed at accounting for linguistic competence. In other words, how do learners develop the system of internalized rules of the language being learned (Ellis, 1986).

Such concern with the intrapersonal dimensions of language development has little to offer our study of the interpersonal dimensions of language, of language in use. The terms "interpersonal" and "use" in this sense are associated with the perspective of the British linguist J.R. Firth, who insisted upon a sociological component in linguistic studies. The foundation for his approach to language is the mutual dependency of language, culture, and society (Firth, 1957; Halliday, 1978; Palmer, 1968), which is well suited to the goals of our study. It is not only evident in our overall approach to investigating the role of English in Europe, but underlies the development of Kachru's world Englishes studies as well (as it does the systemic/functional linguistics of Michael Halliday [1978]).

The Firthian approach, while not identified as the basis for current orientations to second language acquisition research (perhaps because it is less associated with second language learning than with first language learning; see, e.g., Halliday 1975), has much in common with the more socially-oriented research we turned to. The latter emphasizes the relationship between learner and social context as one that is reflexive and constantly changing. Environmental factors are taken into account as influences on second language learning; among these factors are attitudes and their role in motivation. Sociocultural theory offers a useful metaphor in this regard: learning *as participation*, which is not a replacement for, but a complement to the traditional metaphor of learning as acquisition. As Lantolf (2000) explains, the new metaphor shifts focus of investigation from language structure to language use in context and to the issues of affiliation and belonging. It further stresses contextualization and engagement with others. Another relevant dimension of sociocultural theory is recognition that languages are continuously remolded by their users to serve their communicative and psychological needs, just as each generation reworks its cultural inheritance to meet the needs of communities and individuals.

This more rounded view of learners as social beings is attractive to us because it allows consideration of dimensions of society; for example, socioeconomic status, opportunities for language use, formal and informal learning, variety exposure, and attitudes toward languages, among others (see Preisler's 1999 study involving these characteristics).

1.3.1 Comprehensible input via media

It is "basic common ground among theorists of language learning" (Mitchell & Myles, 1998, p.14) that it is necessary to interpret and to process incoming language data in some form for normal language development. These incoming data (*input*) are useless, however, unless they are also comprehensible (Swain, 1985), and thus, accessible, for cognitive processing.

Of direct relevance to our investigation are studies that have identified television as a source of comprehensible input (see Garza, 1991; MacWilliam, 1986; Tudor, 1987; Vanderplank, 1999). Watching television uniquely enhances proficiency in second language skills because of the greater cognitive investment of the L2 learners in the act of viewing (Meskill, 1998). Further, television viewing is an activity that implies a level of comprehension on the part of viewers regardless of any unfamiliarity with the language and culture depicted (Garza 1991, p.78). Persons with limited skills in that language and culture have at their disposal a repertoire of viewing literacy skills that can assist their decoding of novel aural input. There is evidence indicating that schemata activated through aural and visual channels do in fact facilitate comprehension of complex linguistic input in a foreign or second language (Mueller, 1980, as cited in Meskill, 1998).

The argument that watching TV is a source of comprehensible input is supported by D'ydevalle & Pavakanun (1997), who suggest that the frequent viewing of subtitled television programs in part gives smaller language communities, for example, Denmark, Dutch-speaking Belgium, and the Netherlands, the advantage of knowing several languages. In Belgium, for example, many children know how to speak and understand a considerable amount of English even before they receive formal English language education. At least in part, this may be due to their watching of television (p. 146). Similarly, it has been suggested that intense contact with media at an early age makes it possible for the learners who begin English curriculum later than their peers to reach the same level of proficiency, but in a shorter period of time (Königs, 1999, p. 255).

1.3.2 Multilingual acquisition

The notion *multilingual acquisition* is a recent addition to second language acquisition studies (Cenoz & Jessner, 2000). It is used to describe the process of acquiring more than two languages, which comprises the consecutive as well as simultaneous acquisition of three or more languages. As such, it is of considerable relevance to our investigation for two reasons. First, it applies to the contemporary linguistic situation of Europe and second it is a correction to the assumption underlying much SLA research, which regards monolingualism as the unmarked case among the learners studied. Researchers assume that the new language will be the learners' second language and will make them at most bilingual.

Multilingual acquisition more aptly describes the reality of the families of immigrants, guest workers, refugees, or bilingual households. In many cases, a language is learned after two or more additional languages have been learned, and it often happens that different languages are learned for different functions and for use in various contexts of situation.

1.3.3 Acquisitional roles of language

In acquisitional terms, English is either a foreign or a second language. Referring to English as a *foreign* language foregrounds it as the first language of British or Americans. As such, its acquisition serves the purpose of making oneself understood by native speakers, while language instruction to some extent includes cultural studies about the respective countries. In general, the term *second* language is used to identify situations in which English is a *language of wider communication* (LWC). That is, it is relevant to a region, gives access to economic development and public life, and is encountered within the local region or community.

Throughout Europe, English has traditionally been taught as a foreign language. However, it functions as a second language by serving as a language of wider communication, and has become the most common means of communication between and among speakers of the various European languages and language varieties. The term *lingua franca,* which once signaled functional or domain restriction of a language, is now often used to describe English in Europe and its role in enabling cross-cultural and cross-linguistic communication.

This designation is useful for our purposes because it obviates the need to argue for English as either a second or foreign language, terms that do not really suit our goals. If taken literally, as it often is, "second" suggests' that the learners in our study are monolingual, while "foreign" implies that the cultural and linguistic reference point is that of the so-called native speakers of Britain or the United States. Neither interpretation applies any longer in Europe (if anywhere), in part due to political, social and economic changes that make boundaries and borders less distinct (begging the question "What is foreign?"), and in part due to the multilingualism that is a sine qua non of a unified Europe and widely regarded as an antidote to the dominance of American English and culture.

1.3.4 Communicative competence and functional proficiency

Inclusion of the notion "communicative competence" from Hymes (1972) and its subsequent interpretations for language pedagogy and assessment (Bachman & Savignon, 1986; Savignon, 1997) in our theoretical framework follows from our interest in language in use. Defined as a person's ability to communicate appropriately and successfully with respect to whom they are interacting, the purpose of the interaction, and the topic of the interaction – whether orally or in writing - communicative competence puts the focus on what a person does with language, rather than knows about language; on functional proficiency rather than mastery of grammatical structures.

Similarly, attention is on the particular communicative competence that a person develops through formal and informal instruction and use of the language. This is no more relevant than in the case of English as lingua franca and the different varieties of this language that have evolved from its various contexts of spread (e.g., the regional varieties of African English, South Asian English, or the national varieties, for example, Indian and Ghanaian English). Each variety has its own standards of appropriateness that determine the communicative competence of its users, and, because these standards are community determined, they are not universal and thus are not applicable to all speakers of a particular language. In other words, these users of English have a linguistic repertoire (from phonology to pragmatics) from which to draw, with choices depending upon the why, with whom, and about what of the interaction. This issue of multiple standards and norms for English directly bears on determinations of proficiency and assessments of learner achievement.

These issues were important in determining our approach to finding out (1) what the learners in our study could do with English, and (2) how their level of proficiency might relate to such affective factors as motivation and attitude.

1.3.5   Attitudes and motivation

Research in social psychology has demonstrated consistent relationships between language attitudes, motivation, and second language achievement (see Gardner, 1985; Gardner & McIntyre, 1993). The basic assumption is that motivation to learn another language is decisive in learning success in terms of the level of proficiency achieved and the communicative competence developed, and that motivation in turn is connected with learner attitude toward the respective second or foreign language speaking community (see also Clément, Gardner & Smythe, 1977a, b). Attitudes toward the target language, its speakers, and the learning context may all play some part in explaining success or lack thereof in acquiring a particular language.

In Gardner and Lambert's (1972) landmark study of motivation, they distinguish between instrumental and integrative motivation. It is generally assumed that Europeans are instrumentally motivated, as their goal is not integration into either British or American culture, but of becoming proficient enough to meet communicative needs should they ever have the opportunity to interact with inner-circle speakers of English. However, as Preisler (1999) found, Europeans can in fact be integratively motivated, as was the case for the young Danes in his study who wanted to learn English, particularly American English, to symbolize their identity, affiliation and solidarity with their peer group and its culture. This has significance for our concentration on youth.

Attitude studies with a different focus are also relevant. Two, one by Flaitz (1988) and one by de Bot and Weltens (1997), stand out because they are bold and rare empirically-based attempts to gain insight into attitudes across socio-economic groups and toward other languages. Flaitz examined attitudes toward English in groups she labeled elite and non-elite in France, and found that the non-elite are more positive toward English than the elites, whose views are more widely publicized and considered as more representative. De Bot and Weltens surveyed the attitudes of speakers of Dutch, English, German and Turkish living in Netherlands toward their own and each others' languages; they found that presuppositions about Dutch speakers as indifferent to their language and as enamored of English for its functionality and international character did not hold for the groups studied. Our study is a continuation of this line of research.

1.4   MEDIA STUDIES

As cultural forums, media create culture and simultaneously transmit representations of other cultures. This is particularly so in broadcast media, where the increasing number of satellite channels, for example, increase the internationalized quality of the media to a high degree. Media influence on the development of social and national identity is also relevant in this regard. The attractiveness of mass media to young people centralizes theories of its effects and impact on acquisition. Media also create culture and play a role in cultural change. Communication theory's rich heritage of media effects research, though controversial and somewhat inconclusive, provides the language scholar with a range of theoretical frameworks for assessing the role of language in media settings (Hasebrink, Berns, & Skinner, 1997).

An important area of concern is the functions of media. The media do more than provide information or entertain, do more than convey knowledge and representations of other cultures or provide an opportunity to have a direct look at the products of another culture. They also play formative role in society by informing, or at a deeper level, by forming, concepts, belief systems and verbal, visual, and symbolic languages that citizens use to make sense of the world and their place in it. Thus, the role of media extends to influencing who we think we are and where we believe we fit (or not) in this world; that is, the media play a major role in forming our cultural identity (Oreja, 1998, p. 9).

1.4.1   Social effects of mass media

One branch of research particularly relevant to this study is that of social effects of mass media. Representative theories are the so-called cultivation theory (Gerbner, 1972; see also Signorielli & Morgan, 1990) and social learning theory (Bandura & Walters, 1963). The cultivation thesis assumes that, over the long term, the patterns of representation in television shape the worldview of viewers. Thus, frequent TV viewers develop ideas about reality that coincide with the patterns seen on TV; at the same time, their views become more similar. These assumptions bear directly on our study of media and the acquisition of English: as the media to a great extent offer Anglo-American pop culture and American entertainment products, the media world that results is shaped by the English language and American cultural patterns. According to social learning theory, also called theory of imitative learning, television viewers acquire new attitudes or modeling behavior simply by observing symbolic role models, without the benefit of direct reinforcement. Both theories suggest that exposure to stereotypes (social and cultural) in the mass media will contribute to the development of stereotypical beliefs, attitudes, and behaviors, and that television plays an important part in the socialization process.

These views focus on what media do to people; another perspective, one that is consistent with the views on language and cultural identity taken in this study, is to attend to what people do with what they get from the media. With the young people in our study, the issue was what they do with both the information conveyed via the media and the language, in this case English, it is presented in and how these processes relate to English proficiency and attitudes. This raises the question of who is in control of the media – the consumer or the originators of media products.

Due to consumer contact with foreign cultures through various media, cultural preservationists and language purists across Europe raise concerns about cultural imperialism and hegemony. These individuals do not value the positive effects of such contact, one of which is a contribution to international communication. Instead, they anticipate the eventual loss of cultural identity and the adoption of worldviews, values and cultural traditions associated with the more powerful media producing cultures – the United States, in particular.

1.4.2   Media and European identities

Hofstede also addresses the future of national identities in this era of international integration, an issue of concern to this study as well. Paraphrasing Hofstede, the questions we would pose are: will English and the American culture associated with it obliterate national mental programs? Is it true that societies, organizations, and groups have ways of conserving and passing on mental programs from generation to generation with an obstinacy that many people tend to underestimate, as Hofstede claims (1980, p. 17)?

This question is particularly relevant to the efforts of the EU to foster and develop a readily identifiable and distinctive European identity through cultural artifacts. First is the creation or valorization of the conscious, visible culture for Europe - symbols, rituals, and heroes. The choice of images for the euro banknotes and coins is one example of deliberate collective programming; the ideas behind the images are described in a brochure of the European Central Bank (1999). On the notes, windows, gateways, and bridges symbolize "the spirit of openness and cooperation in Europe." These elements depict the architectural styles of seven periods in Europe's cultural history. The images on the coins represent both common and individual symbols. The design on one side is common to all countries; the other side represents national identities with images of persons and structures, art, music, or nature, to name just a few. The euro symbol (€) itself was inspired by the Greek epsilon and refers to the first letter of the word Europe. These symbols are intended to both reflect and shape a European identity, one that may or may not be believed in (see European Commission, 1999).

As the foregoing suggests, culture and identity are presented as concepts referring more or less to the same thing. In discussions on the future of Europe, the emergence of a European culture and identity are often presented as being almost similar. Perhaps from a distance it looks as if Europeans share the same culture, but from within Europe the differences appear to be more relevant than that which is held in common. The French feel they are very different from Norwegians and vice-versa. At the same time, many Europeans will feel some sort of European identity, in particular when confronted with, say, expressions of American or Japanese identity. Yet, it is likely that a new type of European culture based on more recent developments is likely to form.

1.5   THE REST OF THE BOOK

It is this rich interdisciplinary framework, constructed from elements of the broad fields of sociolinguistics, second language acquisition research, and culture and media studies that guides our investigation. The next seven chapters, written by different authors or combinations of authors, lay out the steps and the strategies used to take up the challenge of bringing cross disciplinary perspectives and preferences together on the question of English in Europe.

We begin in Chapter 2, with a composite sociolinguistic profile of English in the four countries where we gathered data - Belgium, France, Germany and the Netherlands. This step not only establishes a context for our study, but also contributes to the theoretical and applied research of world Englishes studies by conjoining hermeneutic and empirical approaches to research. Chapter 3 outlines our empirical approach and details the study design and methodology including basic assumptions that guided the inquiry, research questions, and a description of the data collection instrument – survey questionnaire – and assessment tools – "can do" scales, proficiency scales, and a vocabulary test.

Chapters 4-6 focus on the findings and analyses. In Chapter 4 we present descriptive findings in four categories corresponding to our data sets: family characteristics; media and other sources of contact with English; attitudes; and English language proficiency. Chapter 5 takes up the question of what influences what with an analysis of how the variables described in the previous chapter are causally related. It also discusses how the large number of variables in the study was managed for the analysis. The exploratory analyses presented in Chapter 6 are intended to draw attention to and increase further understanding of how young people use various media to construct individual media environments.

In Chapter 7, we summarize how the findings contribute to our understanding of the "presence" of English, discuss the consequences of its presence for with respect to the current social, cultural and political issues, and consider approaches for future research that would address these issues and the challenging questions they raise.

Chapter 2

ENGLISH IN EUROPE

Margie Berns, Marie-Thérèse Claes, Kees de Bot, Riet Evers, Uwe Hasebrink, Ineke Huibregtse, Claude Truchot, and Per van der Wijst

2.1   INTRODUCTION

A means of gaining insight into the present status, role, and functions of English in a particular social and cultural context is that of the sociolinguistic profile. Frequently used in world Englishes scholarship, following Kachru (1985) and Berns (1990), this framework takes into account both the users and the uses of the language and brings together its historical context, domains of use, role in the educational system, influence on the media, levels of proficiency, and attitudes toward it among learners and users. In the broadest sense, a profile documents the presence of the language and the breadth and depth of its presence. As these concerns in part motivated our inquiry, we have drawn a sociolinguistic profile of English in Europe to contextualize and establish a background for the empirical study described and reported on in Chapters 3-7.

Before turning to the profile of English, a look at Europe's linguistic diversity and changing language demographics is in order because it is against this backdrop that the present and future of English, which is tied to the other languages of Europe, can be better understood.

2.2   EUROPEAN LINGUISTIC DIVERSITY

Europe is diverse in many aspects, and language is not the least of them. Fifty distinct languages are recognized across Europe, including Russia and Turkey - 33 as official state languages and 17 as officially recognized regional languages. This number, as reported by Trim (1994, cited in Lambert 1994), does not include spoken varieties or languages brought by immigrants. There are also over 40 "small" languages – as they are often called – spoken by over 40 million people. France, for example, has speakers of Basque, Breton, Catalan, Corsican, and Occitan. Spoken elsewhere are Albanian, Breton, Cornish, Croatian, Danish, Franco Provencal, Friulan, Galician, Irish, Langue d'Oc, Low German, Luxembourgian, Macedonian, Romany, Turkish, Welsh, and Yiddish, among others. Although Belgium, with Dutch, French and German as official state languages, does not confer official status on any regional or minority language, a distinction can be made among regional dialects, such as Walloon, Gaumais, and Picardy.

Patterns of immigration also contribute to the linguistic landscape across Europe. Open borders, mobility for study and work, and changes due to political and economic developments in Central and Eastern Europe and in other regions of the world have introduced new languages. A variety of immigrant languages, Italian, Arabic, Spanish, Turkish, and Portuguese, for example, are found in present-day Belgium. Industrialized France and Germany provide additional examples. In France there are now speakers of the immigrant languages found in Belgium -- Italian, Arabic, Spanish, Portuguese, others such as Berber, Creole, and, more recently, Turkish, in addition to a variety of African and Asian languages. In Germany, a majority of those of school age have been the children of workers who have come from Turkey, the new Balkan states, Italy, and Greece; another important group is made up of immigrants from Asian countries.

. Germany's linguistic diversity is also represented by the languages used as the medium for instruction and the place of minority languages in the school curriculum. As 90 % of Germany's population is ethnic German, the language of instruction is German, the only official state language. An exception is Sorbian, a minority/regional language with official language status in the Länder of Brandenburg and Saxony. It serves as the medium in either a total immersion or partial immersion arrangement from primary to either post-compulsory or upper-secondary education (European Commission, 2001). Danish and Frisian, the other two minority languages (only Danish has official status), are offered only as a school subject – Danish in Schleswig-Holstein, and Frisian in Lower Saxony and Schleswig-Holstein. Turkish, the language of 2.5% of Germany's population, is not offered as a school language, but is used in separate after school lessons for Turkish children.

The complexity and dynamics of such linguistic diversity in Europe have assigned English unique positions. The immigrant populations and minority groups, in particular, necessitate recognition of English as a third language, as discussed in Cenoz and Jessner (2000). This is the case for immigrants when English is a compulsory first foreign language in school and as such takes its place behind the official language of the new country, which serves as a second language. At the same time, their native language is used at home. English also is a third language for European speakers of such minority autochthonous languages as Basque, Breton, Sardinian, Catalan, Frisian and Sàmi.

They also have the majority language as the second language and learn English as a third language. Such speakers include Spanish children who learn Catalan or Basque at school, native speakers of Dutch who learn Frisian at school, native speakers of Dutch in Belgium, who learn French as a second language, and native speakers of Swedish in Vaasa/Vasa who learn Finnish and English. Yet other examples are native speakers of widespread European languages whose language is a minority one at the national level and who also learn English as a third language, for example, German speakers in France, Italy, or Belgium.

2.2.1 Historical context of English

The breadth and depth of the spread of English throughout Europe today belies its comparatively limited influence up to the 20th century. The language of the British Isles was little used outside its shores between 1375 and 1550, when the English were prosperous and commercially independent. This does not mean that England had no contact with the continent during that time or even earlier. Although England and France had significant points of contact prior to the 12th century, it is in the 17th and 18th centuries that English gained influence across the English Channel. In fact, it was claimed (although not the case) that during the 18th century English was almost universally understood in Holland, "kindly entertained as a relation in the most civilized parts of Germany," and studied, "tho' yet little spoke" as a learned language in France and Italy (Stanhope, 1777, in Bailey 1991, p. 99). For France, Britain's development of economic and political liberalism in the second half of the 18th century in part played a role in facilitating interest in the English language. English's earliest period of significant influence on Germany began in the mid-17th century and continued into the late-18th century. By the 19th century English had gradually spread farther across Europe to the extent that it had become "esteemed an essential" in Russia and Scandinavia as well as Germany (A.C.C., 1829, cited in Bailey, 1991, p.107).

In the 20th century English assumed a stronger presence in Europe, and not solely due to British influence. The United States' part in ending the First World War and its new standing as a world power are attributed to a linguistic innovation introduced in 1919 with the Peace Treaty of Versailles. Up to that time, treaties had been written in French in keeping with its traditional role in the domain of diplomacy; the Versailles treaty had both English and French versions. The influence of the United States became more marked after 1945, and American English eventually became a significant feature of secondary education – and eventually primary education - in Europe after the 1950's. Further developments in the second half of the 20th century also strengthened the hold of English in Europe. Among them were the influx of American and British popular music in the 1960s and more widespread use of English among scientists in the 1970s. The UK also joined the Common Market in the 1970's, thus increasing Britain's role in the displacement of French as the only official language of the Market's successor, the European Union.

Curriculum reform in Germany during this decade allotted English a larger role in the education of children of all ability levels. Previously, English instruction was reserved for the most "able," who would continue their education beyond Grade 10 and become the elite in society. Increased availability of textbooks, training manuals, and research reports in English rather than German, and contacts with English-speaking coworkers and clients meant that young Germans going into technological, industrial, or commercial fields would need English (Berns, 1990). The Netherlands followed suit in the 1980's. English was made a compulsory subject in the last two years of primary education, and the only compulsory language for all types of secondary education, including vocational training. A flashpoint in this time frame was the Dutch Minister of Education's public statement that English should be used more widely in universities, which caused a major uproar. Parliament immediately asked questions, the minister insisted that he did not intend to have Dutch replaced by English, and discussion on the role of English in academia ensued. More generally, it was in the latter half of the 1980s that English was given a larger role in multinational companies, a practice that expanded during the 1990s.

The effect of these developments was experienced differently from place to place. The impact was perhaps most dramatic in Germany after the Soviet Union closed the eastern German border to western Germany in 1952 and built the Berlin Wall in 1961. These two actions effectively cut off contact with the west for one third of the country and a sector of Berlin, thus isolating the Germans living there from western influences, including English.

Belgium's complex linguistic situation also involves the establishment of a different type of political border (Witte, Craebeckx & Meynen, 1997). Tensions among French- and Dutch-speaking Belgians going back at least to the 13th century were caused by and contributed to alternating periods of prestige and power for each language (Wils, 1992). In the 20th century, two sets of laws were passed that determined the country's linguistic future from the 1960s onwards. One set fixed the linguistic border, which had been flexible; the other resulted in laws concerning the use of languages in education, administration, and justice. Flanders was most affected as there were to be no French-speaking schools; the impact was less in Wallonia, which had no Dutch-speaking schools. During this period, French was considered the language of education and culture and had become more prestigious. Brussels, the capital, had become more French speaking. Although English is part of the language mix and is a means of international communication for contemporary Belgians, its role is less contentious and its history is relatively insignificant compared to that of either Dutch or French.

In 21st century Europe, as in most other regions of the world, English is used for a variety of purposes and serves its speakers in a range of functions and domains. It dominates in the fields of science and technology, diplomacy and international relations, sports and international competitions, media (audio, visual, electronic, print), business and commerce, design and fashion, travel and tourism, the entertainment industry, and higher education.

One of the most widespread functions of English is as an international language among those involved in cross-national and international business and affairs on a global level. At the local European level, English is a link language at the highest levels of official international communication, for example, the United Nations or the European Union. The linking function is also realized in daily personal use among colleagues over dinner after a professional or scholarly meeting, co-workers in the office of a multinational company, or families on vacation making the acquaintance of local residents or other vacationers. It is also a vehicle of creative and imaginative expression through the linguistic processes of nativization, which is observable in both spoken and written texts and in various genres. Texts in which innovative uses of English frequently appear are advertising copy, public postings and announcements, and advertising spots on television, radio, and the internet. Journalism is often a locus for innovation and play with English. It is also identified as serving a symbolic function, or a marker of status and prestige. The use of English to name firms and brands, for example, conveys an international image.

2.2.2 English in the workplace

In this section we consider more generally the role of English in the workplace, one domain in which contact with and use of it are pervasive. In particular we look at the fields of business and commerce (including advertising) and of science and technology, two areas of activity where extensive contact with English is increasingly unavoidable.

English is strongly promoted in workplace Europe. Banks in Switzerland use English at the senior level; English has been adopted in Swedish boardrooms, and even though its staff is only 10% British, English is the official language of the European Central Bank located in Frankfurt, Germany. At professional meetings and conferences English is the most used working language. An estimated 99% of European organizations listed in a yearbook of international associations assign it this role as well (Crystal, 1997, cited in Graddol, 1997, p. 8).

Specialized languages have been created for various occupations. PoliceSpeak, a restricted language operational in both English and French and a set of procedures for police communication, was especially created for law enforcement officers on each side of the frontier and is used frequently as a lingua franca at meetings by police personnel at all levels and ranks, especially in countries using more than two languages. AirSpeak, an air traffic pilot training communication program, has been developed for use internationally by air traffic control, cockpit, and ground crews. SeaSpeak was created to regulate maritime communication in international waters and in port (see Johnson, 2000; Ingleton, 1994).

Evidence of the requirements for English is postings for positions in a variety of vocations and professions that call for knowledge of English where high levels of proficiency can be required for telephone and internet communications, face-to-face meetings, and written correspondence and documents. As a study by Truchot (2001) suggests, the demand for English is strong in the French workplace. He found that in the French daily paper, Le Monde, 70 % of the jobs posted on average had language requirements; ninety-five percent specified a high level of competence in English as a qualification. In Belgium, the competence called for in any language includes not only knowledge about the language, but also ability to use the language, with stress on oral communication. Flemish companies are particularly rigorous when it comes to languages. Prospective employees have to be highly proficient in Dutch first, then French, followed by English and German. In the Netherlands, job announcements implicitly assume potential employees' English skills and only mention English proficiency when very special skills or near-native command is necessary. Even more striking are job advertisements (in English) which explicitly state that proficiency in Dutch is not required.

Employees themselves, as Biersack, Dostal, Parmentier, Plicht, & Troll (1998/99) found, regard English knowledge as only modestly important. Asked for their view about personal needs for further education, employees in services and administrative sectors regarded foreign languages, by a wide margin, as second in importance. Further education in computer skills ranked first.

2.2.2.1 Business and commerce

The business environment is extremely international, and English is an important part of a global participant's linguistic repertoire. Multinationals have their European headquarters in major cities in different countries. In the Netherlands, English is the daily language in most international companies, also among speakers of Dutch (Nickerson, 2000). Sometimes this is a formal policy to underscore the international flavor of the company;

other times English is used in internal communication, like email, because one individual in the communicative chain may not be a native speaker of Dutch. According to Truchot (2001), the practice of institutionalizing English as a company language was reported as early as the 1970s in the Nordic countries; yet the first well-known example in France is that of Airbus Industries in the 1980s, when English was given an official status in its branches in France and Germany as well as Britain and Spain. As Truchot reports, in what language or languages internal linguistic communication took place is not known and itself merits study (see Denis, 1999; Coppieters 't Wallant, 1997: Verluyten, Thiré & Demarest, 1999 on business needs in Belgium).

Marketers and advertisers exploit English to reach an international audience and to lend cachet to the products and services they sell. In fact, advertisers have been explicitly advised to do so because, in de Mooij's (1994) words, "the better-educated throughout Europe as well as the youth can be reached with English" (p. 288). In the Netherlands, English is present in various forms of advertising, which has been identified as the forefront of the spread of English (see Gerritsen, 1995; Gerritsen, Korzilium, van Meurs, & Gijsbers, 1999). A 1999 study by Gerritsen, van Meurs, & Gijsbers inventoried TV commercials in which English is used and found that about a third of the commercials were either partly or completely in English. Common in advertising is the use of English words for the connotative value, a fairly old practice (Truchot, 1990). The association of English with certain aesthetic qualities can transfer these desirable qualities to its users or a product. Thus, such words and phrases as "Happy Hour," "Kids," "Summertime-Playtime," and "Soft am Body" appear in clothing ads in Germany. Such use is said to convey an air of modernity and progress, to sell a lifestyle as well as a set of values and attitudes.

English lexical items are not necessarily more numerous today, but recent empirical observations of French practices do indicate that they are more elaborate, which might suggest that advertisers take it for granted that knowledge of English has risen. Martin (2002b) concluded from her study of English in media advertising in France that the use of English is still a favored strategy in print and on television. Her findings also indicate that the variety of English most often heard in French television commercials is some form of American English (see also Martin 2002a; Martin & Hilgendorf, 2001). In Germany, too, the use of English is a prevalent strategy for capitalizing on the English language's assumed association with things modern and its cachet with young people. However, this belief in the advantages of English in advertising has not been supported by empirical studies on audiences. For example, Gawlitta (2001), in an investigation on the acceptance of English-language advertising slogans, found that older target groups widely dislike English slogans and that even young people do not really like Anglicisms in advertising.

2.2.2.2 Science and technology

The highly internationalized nature of such fields as science and technology is a basis for the use of English. Competence in English, both in written and spoken communication, is becoming a linguistic sine qua non among researchers in these fields. Truchot's (1997) study of this reality among French scientists seems representative of the situation elsewhere in Europe. The findings offer insights into the place of English in professional publications and conferences that illustrate the extent and nature of the language situation in these areas.

French scientists, like all other scientists in the world, have to use English as a language of publication if they want their research to be most widely disseminated. The nature of publishing contributes to this situation. More than 80 % of the journals that make the "hard core" of scientific communication are owned by a handful of multinational publishing companies and are issued almost entirely in English. The articles they publish are used as references everywhere and are indexed before all others in the scientific databases. The largest, most widely used and most influential of these is located in the USA, the Science Citation Index, or SCI. Some 90 % of the information recorded in these databases comes from contributions written in English; the remaining 10 % is shared among Russian, French, German, and Japanese. In European databases, the space allocated to European languages other than English is hardly larger. As a consequence, most of the scientific journals in Germany, France and Italy have turned to English as the language of publication. Lists of publications provided by applicants to professorships in the hard sciences are similarly revealing: almost all are articles placed in American, British and European journals published in English. Some 20 years ago such lists would have given equal share to English and French titles.

English is the main language used at conferences in France, too. A survey commissioned by the Délégation Générale à la Langue Française (DGLF, 1998) showed that out of 102 international scientific conferences which took place in France in 1997, 53 % had English as their only official language and 32 % English together with other languages. The organizers of these conferences generally use French together with English in publicity and external communication, a practice required by a 1994 language law. However, according to scientists, doing so appears to be a habit that serves a mostly symbolic function.

There are two settings within the French scientific community where English seems to be used less than in other countries. One is for personal communication in the places where science is produced, such as laboratories and research centers. There researchers tend to communicate in French, even if they are from several language backgrounds. An exception is short-term visitors, with whom communication often takes place in English.

There are a number of published French language studies and summaries used by researchers to take stock of their discipline as a whole in relation to their particular specialization or to obtain information about other disciplines. Examples are the journals *Médecine-Sciences* and *Comptes-rendus de l'Académie des Sciences*. English is also used less in popular scientific publications for the larger public, for example, the monthly review *La Recherche*.

In addition, efforts are made to maintain an up-to-date and comprehensive scientific and technical terminology in French, a practice not necessarily followed in Germany or the Netherlands where English names for processes, tools, and concepts are more readily adopted.

The place of English in research in other EU states has been investigated by German in the sciences. Two studies in particular that have dealt with this issue extensively are those by Skudlik (1990) and Ammon (1998). Skudlik demonstrates that all fields of inquiry are not equally dependent upon English for communication and divides them into three categories: anglophone sciences (physics, chemistry and some parts of medicine), anglophone influenced sciences (veterinary medicine, forestry, economics, psychology, linguistics) and sciences influenced by national languages and/or multilingual sciences (law, pedagogy, archeology, theology and some branches of cultural studies). Ammon (1998) considers the role of German as an international language of science and English as the medium of instruction at German in higher education and training (see also Carli & Calaresu (2003) on the language of scientific communication and the production and diffusion of specialist knowledge in Italy).

2.3 ENGLISH IN EDUCATION

English is the most taught language in virtually every country of the European Union (Eurydice, 2005). Formerly it was taught primarily for integrative purposes with the expectation that learners would become proficient in English solely to interact with British subjects. As this is no longer tenable in multilingual and multicultural Europe, where English is a lingua franca for interactions between and among speakers of various non-English language backgrounds, the broad and encompassing goal for classroom learning is the communicative competence that is useful with other English learners and users like themselves within and beyond Europe. This goal does not replace that of familiarity with and appreciation of the language and culture of Britain, which remains important for the purposes of

European integration. Both orientations, the instrumental and integrative, are part of the primary and secondary school curricula across Europe.

2.3.1   Primary and secondary education

Foreign language instruction may be either mandatory or optional, depending upon the country. In 13 EU countries learning English is mandatory (which means that 90% of school age learners learn it ahead of other languages). When learners have a free choice, 90% of them opt for English (Eurydice, 2005). In France, the Flemish Community of Belgium, Germany, and the UK (except in Scotland), a first foreign language is compulsory for all pupils from the start of secondary education, usually at age 10, and continues for all pupils to the end of their compulsory education. A second foreign language may be required at lower secondary level, as it is in Belgium (the Flemish Community), Finland, Greece, and the Netherlands; in Portugal and Spain it is a compulsory option. In Austria, France, and Germany other criteria, such as the particular school attended, determine the learning of language (Eurydice, 2001).

Instructional hours vary across school level. In the earlier grades in Germany, for instance, English lessons are given two hours per week, then increase to an average of three and a half hours for 13-year olds, and can reach a maximum of five hours per week for 16 year-olds (European Commission, 2001a). Language instruction generally ends at Grade 10 for those who do not go on for three more years of schooling at the Gymnasium. In the Netherlands, an estimated 92% of all pupils follow English lessons with a modal number of 150 minutes a week. As a rule, most learners have a total of eight years of language instruction (including, but not limited to English).

Usually, English is required as one, if not the only, first compulsory language, or is the most frequently selected among language options. One exception is Belgium. In Flanders the first foreign language has to be French; Wallonia, however, gives choices: Dutch, English, and German; in Brussels, the first compulsory foreign language in French-speaking schools is Dutch, and vice versa in the Dutch-speaking schools.

Overall, English, French, and German are taught in Belgian primary schools starting in grade 5 and onwards; Spanish and Italian, along with English are offered at the secondary level. In Flanders, where French is their first foreign language, English is not part of primary education but is at secondary level. English classes begin at the second stage for two to three periods a week. With some exceptions, students are free to select their first foreign language from among Dutch, German or English. English is taught as a foreign language from the second year on. In the officially bilingual Brussels Region, education is monolingual – the medium is either French or

Dutch. However, instruction in either Dutch or French (the second language) is mandatory from Grade 3 onwards. At the secondary level in Wallonia a second foreign language is optional in the third year. In vocational secondary education, English is compulsory three times a week for majors in marketing and management, with English (and French) recommended for others. In the fine arts track, only some pupils have English at the second and third stages. For those on the technical track, English is compulsory twice a week, with additional one to two periods per week if they are majors in commerce and languages.

There is a steady trend in Europe toward teaching languages more widely at the primary level. The recommendations of the Barcelona Council in March, 2002 that languages should be taught at an increasingly younger age appear to be having an effect (Eurydice, 2005). At least half of all primary learners get instruction in one foreign language in the great majority of countries (Eurydice, 2005). In 1989 France introduced foreign language education in primary schools for one and one-half hours per week; today 100% of the children have foreign language classes. As of the 1994-1995 school year, 79.8% of primary learners were taking English as the second foreign language (cf. 15.2 % for German and 3% and 2% for Spanish and Italian, respectively) (Eurydice, 1997; Eurostat, 1997; Ministère de L'éducation Nationale, 2000). In the 1990s some German states began offering a few hours of language instruction per week as early as Grade 1 at all basic education schools. The majority learn English, except in the regions which border France, where French is taught. Even pre-school foreign language instruction is available on a limited basis in Germany. In the Netherlands, English is a compulsory subject in the last two years of primary education.

2.3.2   Bilingual education and English medium schools

Across Europe, education through the medium of another language is available in private as well as public schools. Known variously as bilingual, multilingual, dual language, immersion, content and language integrated/CLIL depending upon the setting and the form in which it is implemented, English is well represented, serving as both a medium and a subject of instruction (see Marsh, Marsland, & Maljers, 1998, for discussion of CLIL).

In a model school in Northern Germany, pupils learn all subjects (except German and Religion) in English (see, for example, Wode, 1998a, b). The introduction of this form of language immersion, an experimental exception in German basic education, began in the 2001-2002 school year with 400 pilot schools. In some regions of Germany, immersion begins the third year in either French or English, in others as early as the first year (Otto, 2000, p.

67). No decisions have yet been made regarding the institution of this model.

Most English medium schools in Belgium are in Brussels and are attended primarily by children of expatriates. The International School of Brussels provides primary through secondary education, and French is taught daily at every level. Intensive instruction in English as an additional language is also available. These schools can be bi- or multilingual. European Schools offer bilingual education in English in the Brussels region as well (Baetens-Beardsmore, 1997). Elsewhere in Belgium, most notably in Wallonia, bilingual education has been implemented.

Foreign languages as a medium of instruction are found mostly at the upper secondary level in France. An exception is the English medium international schools with private primary and secondary education that were opened for residents coming from English-speaking countries. Some mainstream French secondary schools also offer special sections with a foreign language as a medium of instruction. In a small number of cases, international sections have been implemented. These *sections internationales* are attended primarily by foreign but also by French pupils aged 6-18. In 1992, European sections were created; the teachers and pupils are French but a foreign language is used for non-linguistic subjects, including science (Dickson & Cumming, 1996). The objective is to facilitate the integration of foreign pupils into both the French school system and that of the home country, in case they return. They likewise seek to create for French pupils an effective learning environment for the advanced study of a foreign language (Eurydice, 2001).

In Germany there are now a number of bilingual primary European schools that partner German with one of the following languages: English, French, Russian, Spanish, Italian, Turkish, Greek, Portuguese, or Polish. Bilingual sections, first introduced in 1969, are predominantly German-English or French-English; at least one other subject in the foreign language is offered. A more recent development in bilingual education is bilingual "wings" or "branches" (*bilinguale Zweige*). Founded in different types of secondary schools (comprehensive, vocational, primary, college preparatory), lessons in content areas begin through the instructional medium in Grade 7. Children in Grades 5 and 6 are prepared seven to eight hours per week for this instruction in intensive foreign language courses that introduce the relevant structures and technical terms needed in subsequent years. Germany has had private international and European schools for some time. Pre-school bilingual education, while not widely available, has been free in Berlin since 1992. Its innovative design integrates bilingual European streams into normal German schools.

What is called bilingual education in the Netherlands means the Dutch-speaking pupils receive education through a foreign language. Beginning as a grass-roots movement by a number of highly-motivated teachers and parents who convinced their schools to start this new line of teaching, it is regarded as a means of improving the efficiency of foreign language teaching in the Dutch secondary school system. Its aim is for the pupils to reach high levels of language proficiency in English. In most schools offering these programs, the second language used is English (attempts to set up bilingual streams using other languages have failed so far).

2.3.3 Higher education: English as subject, English as medium

A domain in which English has an increasingly significant role is higher education, in part due to the increasing internationalization of education and mobility of students seeking advanced degrees throughout the world. It seems to dominate both as a (often required) subject and as a medium of instruction even though other languages are offered and/or are designated as the language of the institution.

In Belgium, learning foreign language continues through tertiary education for most students as language programs are frequently compulsory. In one study, Verluyten, Thiré & Demarest (1994) found that 98% of students in Flanders studied French, 95% studied English, 72% studied German, while only 14% and 3% respectively studied Spanish and Italian. Students considered French (81%) and English (80%) equally important, with these languages the first choice. In Wallonia, further study of languages appears to be limited to some faculties, such as economics and business administration. English is less common because universities are predominantly oriented toward the Francophone academic community. English language instruction is offered at the institutions' language centers, but university courses are rarely English medium. The French-speaking institutions do participate in international programs, but the partners have a mainly Roman, not an Anglo-Saxon, background. Foreign students are expected to be able to attend courses given in French and the institutions provide extensive French language training for students who need it (see Berlamont, 2002; Delbeke, 2002: Devreese, 2002 on the role of English in higher education in Belgium).

In Dutch higher education, English is taught at six universities. In addition, English is taught in various other programs, such as American Studies, European Studies, and Business Communication Studies. As in other types of education, the number of students of English exceeds those studying the other major languages.

In France, schools and universities granting diplomas in management, government, and engineering offer several language classes. Learning a foreign language tends to be compulsory for most degrees, with English usually having a privileged position although learning other languages is also encouraged. Though the demand for English is important, the share of other languages seems to develop more quickly.

In Europe, student mobility is now of paramount importance to universities, and each wants to attract foreign students for their degree programs and possibly further research.

One particular consequence of this active recruitment of foreign students is a linguistically diverse study body that is not necessarily uniformly and highly proficient in the local language. At many institutions the presence of just one such student in class can prompt the professor to switch to a language common to all, often English. These developments are reinforced with assigned readings of research reports and scholarship that are published and available only in English. This trend extends to the collections of university libraries, which as a consequence of budget reductions have to limit the number of new acquisitions; when funding is reduced, priority is given to major international publications – thousands of which have 95% of their articles written in English (Bollag, 2000; Treanor, 2000).

The weight given publications in English is reflected in an evaluation made of psychology departments in the Netherlands some years ago by the review committee of NOW/ Nederlandse Organisatie voor Wetenschappelijk Onderzoek (the Dutch national science foundation). This body decided not to consider as research productivity publications written in Dutch, which remarkably did not stir the academic world at all. In contrast, action by another group, the review committee for educational research, did cause a bit of a stir: this group took the step of recognizing publications only in English, which lead to (ineffective) protests because traditionally the Netherlands has always had strong relations with Germany and France on matters related to teaching and education (see also Motz, 2005 on the question of English or German as the language for courses in higher education; Ammon & McConnell, 2002 on English as an academic language in Europe in general).

2.3.4   The Bologna Declaration

A development with considerable impact on the language situation in higher education is the Bologna Declaration of a European Space for Higher Education (Confederation, 2001). It aims to increase the international competitiveness of European higher education in response to changes and challenges related to the "growth and diversification of higher education" and expansion of transnational education. One strategy is the introduction of common diplomas in EU member states.

Although the Declaration stresses the need to achieve its goal within the framework of the diversity of languages, the decree, according to van Dinter and Stappaerts (2002), suggests the possibility of using English for the bachelor's and master's degrees. The special role of English has been acknowledged in action plans from signatory countries. For example, attracting foreign students to a technical university in the Czech Republic is linked to the need for parallel English language courses (Polak, 2000), and the German Minister of Education and Cultural Affairs refers to the increasing numbers of study programs taught in English playing a role in easing the integration of foreign students into the German system.

In the Netherlands, intentions to prepare students for an international career (using English both for speaking and writing) and the popularity of student exchange programs at the European level (notably through Socrates, the European Community's action program in the field of education) inevitably enhance a trend toward an increase in the number of courses taught in English. Recognizing that students from abroad have no intention of learning Dutch to an advanced level of proficiency, Dutch universities, if they are to attract students from various countries, have to use English as a medium of instruction. This strategy has been successful in recent years to the extent that students from Southern Europe now come to the Netherlands. One reason given for their choice is that the English used there is adapted to second language learners rather than native speaker students (and is therefore easier that in English speaking countries).

A German Academic Exchange Service (DAAD/Deutscher Akademischer Austausch Dienst) guide on opportunities for postgraduate studies in Germany asked readers to note that a good knowledge of English, and possibly French and Spanish as well, might be required in some courses, and that some postgraduate courses would be entirely run in English (DAAD, 2003). In the International Degree Program available at several German institutions of higher education, many courses are given in English. Applicants are required to have a good knowledge of English as demonstrated by internationally recognized tests of English (including the American English-based TOEFL). Basic knowledge of German is described as "helpful." Business administration is one field in which English is increasingly necessary. Although a Masters of Business Administration degree (MBA) was relatively unknown in Germany until fairly recently, it is the degree of choice with German students wishing to compete in the international marketplace and work with firms that put a premium on this degree. Of the over 40 MBA programs established in response to this need, two-thirds are taught in English.

English is a medium of instruction in French universities in the sciences, especially at the doctoral level. In other fields, such as business studies and engineering, a high level of proficiency in English is requisite, and being taught through the language is considered the best means to acquire it. Although use of English up to now in the French classroom has been more limited than in the Netherlands, or even Germany (Ammon, 2001), this may change with the Bologna process. In question is whether the linguistic impact experienced there will be similar in French universities. At present, most of the courses offered to foreign students take place in French, a practice which does not seem to deter their enrollment. France has been the second destination (after the UK) chosen by students taking part in the Socrates program (Truchot, n.d.).

2.3.5   Community and workplace education and training

In addition to the learning opportunities provided by primary, secondary, and higher education, both public and private options are available for English study outside these institutions. Many employers (including banks, insurance companies, and harbor authorities) provide special courses for their own personnel and gear the instruction towards the needs of that group. While many non-subsidized, private options for English courses often target the business sector, tuition for other groups is offered through such agencies as the British Council or community continuing education centers, such as the German Volkshochschulen, which give courses in a variety of subjects, including English, to young and old. In the Netherlands, a wide range of institutions, some sponsored by local or national authorities, some working purely on a commercial basis, offer English courses for all levels, professions and ages.

2.4   ENGLISH IN THE MEDIA

In Europe, the media are well established and available in all forms – to a greater or lesser extent - to most Europeans. English appears to be equally established and available in all media forms. In the music world of Belgium, songs in English, even by Belgians, sound more "stylish" to young people (Van der Linden, 2001), and also attractive are such names of television shows such as (Blind Date, Big Brother, or Now or Never). Television news for young people in Wallonia is even called "les Niouzz" (pronounced "news"). The status English has in music is well illustrated by its dominance in the Eurovision Song Contest in 2001. In that year this event, which brings performers from all European countries together, was conducted that year exclusively in English, except for the singer representing France.

2.4.1   Television and film

Exposure to English via entertainment media goes beyond music; the television and film industries contribute to opportunities for Europeans to have contact with English also. Increasingly, the world market for these cultural products is concentrated around Hollywood. According to a 1999 United Nations Development Program/UNDP, scarcely 30% of Hollywood's revenue in 1980 came from abroad compared with 50% nearly 20 years later (cited in *Le Monde*, 13 July 1999). In 1996, 70% of the film market in Europe was claimed by the US, 83% in Latin America, and 50% in Japan. The European Audiovisual Observatory (2001) noted that in the year 2000, the market share of American films had again risen in the 15 countries of the European Union, while that of European films had fallen to 22.5% with strong national variations.

Against the background of these figures, the following section reviews the place of television and film in and language in Europe. Particular attention is given to dubbing and subtitling practices, media markets, and linguistic requirements, language- and culture-related issues and concerns common across Europe. These three topics also provide a framework for identifying variations of the impact of English in film and television across countries.

2.4.2   Media market and linguistic requirements

As in the discussions of English in other sections of this chapter, the media landscape of Europe cannot be painted with a broad brush. Germany, for example, with about 83 million people, has the largest media market in Europe. Consequently, the media landscape has a high concentration of national, German language media. In contrast to Belgium, Switzerland, or the Netherlands, for example, television programs from abroad, such as CNN or BBC World, do not attain substantial market shares. With regard to free television the German market is the most competitive in Europe. Due to high cable (57%) and satellite (30%) distribution, most German households can receive around 25 national channels. As a consequence, the audience market is quite fragmented; in recent years the market leader (RTL/Radio Télévision Luxembourg) reached a share of less than 15 %.

With multiple media landscapes, Belgium is distinguished from other countries. Of the three Belgian Communities, Flanders and Wallonia provide illustrations here (the German Community, due to its small size, will not be included). To begin with, there is a clear split between media offerings for these two parts of the country, including the most obvious difference of Dutch or French language. Each has developed a dual broadcasting system, including two public service channels and several private channels. In addition to the national channels in Belgium, which is one of the most densely cabled countries in the world, people can watch programming from neighboring countries as well as other European countries, for example, Italy or Spain. Supplementing its 25 broadcast stations are the English language programming of the BBC, CNN, or National Geographic, among others. In Flanders alone there are five English language cable stations (Goethals, 1997, p. 107). However, with regard to market shares, the most important foreign channels are those with the respective language: French channels in Wallonia and Dutch channels in Flanders. Wallonian viewers, in particular, devote substantial parts of their viewing time to channels from France (see de Bens & Ross, 2002, pp. 217-220; Hasebrink & Herzog, 2002, p. 123).

D'Haenens (2001, p. 134) found that satellite programming in Western European countries shows an abundance of English language channels and that this continues to increase. However, the linguistic requirements for television are not the same as those for films shown in cinemas. According to Parker (1995), satellites can supply programs and advertising instantaneously in 24 western European languages, but television viewers—as market surveys on several occasions have shown—want television in their own language. This requirement probably explains why the content of TV programs has developed as it has. While U.S. TV serials dominated programs in the 1980s, nowadays quite a few successful TV films or programs are produced locally.

An example is the case of MTV Europe and its concentration on English language pop music, which at the beginning of the 1990s looked as if it were to become a trans-European channel. This perspective changed substantially in the course of the decade. One reason was the launch of the German channel VIVA, which was exclusively dedicated to the promotion of music by Germans (although not necessarily with German language lyrics!). The presenters, or VJs (video jockeys), were young Germans, speaking a German mixed with English words and idioms from the globalized world of pop music. Since the German produced VIVA proved to be more successful than American produced MTV, which changed its strategy and introduced German language programs with German presenters as well. Thus, even in this specific segment of music television for young people, it is still rather difficult to reach large audiences through the English language alone.

2.4.3   Dubbing and subtitling practices

Language dubbing and subtitling are also practiced differently depending upon the country. Larger countries like France and Germany consider the investment in dubbing English-language films worthwhile. Thus, contact via television with exclusively English language offers is a rare occurrence. The countries that dub English language TV programming and films, and which have comparatively low levels of second language knowledge, consequently have a media landscape that in large part is self-referential.

Smaller countries, for example, Portugal, Sweden, and the Netherlands, subtitle films; Scandinavia and the Netherlands, as reported by Hasebrink & Herzog, regard dubbing as "cultural barbarism" (2002, p. 24-25). This means that TV is an important source of contact with foreign languages; in the Netherlands alone, it involves the viewers of the eight million plus televisions the Dutch own. Informal counts show that 40 to 60 % of the programs on Dutch-speaking channels are actually in a foreign language, mainly English. In addition to such popular English language channels as MTV and the Discovery Channel, Dutch TV viewers will get at least one hour of English on average every day. Earlier research (de Bot, Jagt, Janssen, Kessels & Schils, 1986) has shown that watching subtitled TV programs does not mean that only the subtitles are attended to: information is drawn both from the spoken language and from the subtitles. Research by the Dutch Broadcasting Association shows that the Dutch population clearly prefers subtitling over dubbing. Keeping up or developing foreign language skills is expressly mentioned as one of the reasons.

In the Walloon Community of Belgium, however, dubbing is preferred, possibly because in Walloon media English has a place that is much less important than in Flanders. The most important reason for this is the rich French media offerings. Being part of the Francophone world, Wallonia has since the rise of cinema depended to a great extent on French productions. Since France had an intensive production of films, the public was used to French actors (and French voices when sound was added to the pictures). The Francophone market was so important that foreign films of possible interest to the Francophone audience were dubbed in spite of additional costs for doing so. In spite of the preference for dubbing in the French-speaking Community, the public broadcaster Radio-Television de la Belgique Francophone (RTBF) does sometimes show a French language dubbed version of a foreign (mostly American) film and the un-dubbed version simultaneously on public channels. Although only 10% watch the un-dubbed original, RTBF feels obliged to offer it as a public service. The commercial broadcaster, RTL, offers viewers dubbed versions only. Thus, the Walloon audience is rarely confronted with English voices, and the advent of cable television has not really changed this French monopoly. Although in the 1980s Walloon viewers gained access to foreign English-speaking channels (BBC and later, MTV and CNN) and Flemish and Dutch channels that generally subtitle their foreign programs, these newcomers could not compete with the offer of the 15 to 20 Francophone channels because the great majority of Walloons prefer watching foreign films or documentaries in a dubbed version. In Flanders, in contrast, viewers have more exposure to English because films on television (and in cinemas) are not dubbed generally, but shown with subtitles.

Music, television and film are not the only media influenced by American cultural products and by English. In the following, we consider the internet, radio, and print media, all of which are similarly rich in opportunities for contact with English, especially for teenagers, the focus of our study. As d'Haenens (2001) has noted, media availability, accessibility, and use are part of curricular and extra-curricular experience and exposure to

English among young people in particular. English-language films, television programming, computer games, music, billboards and magazines as well as newspapers all provide exposure to English outside of school and contribute to the further spread of English.

2.4.4   Internet, radio and print media

The internet is undoubtedly the fastest-growing communication tool known to the world. The personal computer has reached a high degree of prominence in Europe, particularly in northern countries (d'Haenens 2001; see also Shapiro, 1999, and Graddol, 1997). Although availability and access to the internet is uneven among Europeans, already in 1998, 37.2 million were internet users (of the 159 million users in the world). More than 10 million were in Germany (21.1 million), France (15.4 million), and Italy (10.6 million). Spain and the Netherlands at that time had fewer, with 5.7 million and 5.1 million, respectively.

This increasingly important medium is obviously an opportunity for contacts with English. Although, compared to the first years of the internet, the dominance of the English language on the web has been decreasing with other countries entering the new medium. Estimates in 2001 said that more than 50% of the internet content is in English (http://www.media-awareness.ca/english/resources/research_documents/statistics/internet/englis h_drops_web.cfm). English-language search engines (Yahoo, HOTBOT) are used widely, more so than local counterparts. However, this by no means implies that over 50 % of the actual use of the internet is devoted to English websites. In line with the concept of "glocalization" (global + local), the actual use of the internet is centered on local, regional, or national agencies which "transform" the global content into locally meaningful information. But it is also not the case that websites are in either one language or another because there are also bilingual (even multilingual) sites. Major Dutch institutions (banks, ministries, or museums), for example, typically have an English section in their homepages.

As in other western countries, radio has a large number of formatted programs broadcast for specific target groups. Those programs especially designed to attract young audiences offer mainly current popular music, a large majority of which has English lyrics. As several studies have indicated, radio programs for young audiences in Germany can offer 95 to 100 % of their music in English language (e.g., for the Berlin market, Wichert, 1997). This corresponds to audience studies which consistently show a strong preference among younger audiences for English language music, although older groups still prefer German pop among popular music in general (e.g., Steinborn, 1992; Hasebrink, 2003). In spite of these clear preferences, public debate continues on the share of German language music in radio programs.

Corresponding to rules in France, which require that 40% of broadcast music has French lyrics, the Organization of German Music Publishers has voted in favor of quotas for German language music.

While English language programs are very common on Dutch television and a host of English spoken channels are available, hardly anyone listens to English language radio stations. Intomart's 2003 measurements of listening to radio (http://www.intomart.nl/default.asp) show that no foreign channels reach the 0.1 % threshold. Even the BBC, which most cable providers offer as part of their package and which the majority of Dutch have access to, apparently does not attract many listeners.

Professional and scholarly publications written exclusively in English, as shown above in the sections on science and technology and on higher education, dominate these international fields. A different type of print media, namely English language press, also has a presence in Europe. For instance, shops specializing in books in English are found in many different areas of Brussels. *The Bulletin*, a "magazine for the English speaker in Brussels" was founded in 1962 by a British expatriate. Billed as "the only Belgian newsweekly magazine in English that provides news and views on the political, economical, social and cultural scene in the Capital of Europe," it counts upwards of 52,000 readers each week (*The Bulletin*, 2005). The press market in Flanders and Wallonia is mainly dominated by Belgian publishers.

International press in English is easy to find. *The Times, The Guardian,* and *The Financial Times* from Britain and the *International Herald Tribune* and *The Wall Street Journal* from the U.S. are available in print as well as online versions. These newspapers are not widely influential because they are generally read by specific target groups (other than expatriates and tourists) that rely on English media, such as those in the areas of business, technology or science. Even among these target groups, the trend in Germany, at least, is towards German language editions of international newspapers, *The Financial Times Deutschland* is the German language versions of Britain's *The Financial Times.*

In France, readers of *LeMonde Diplomatique* can access an English edition via its website (www.monde-diplomatique.fr). This monthly publication has editions in several languages, including English. *Pariscope*, a weekly official Parisian guide to TV, cinema, theater, and museum events has a section in English. *France Now* is a monthly magazine reviewing French political, economic, financial, and legal news for the English speaker. A magazine for English-speaking Parisians is *Paris Free Voice Magazine.*

2.4.5   Media functions

Given the availability of local media in the local language, what purposes do English language media serve the European reader, viewer, or web surfer? Is it only to practice the language or to get information or to be entertained? Hasebrink (2001) has proposed that English also serves as a cultural bridge to the individual cultures associated with it. Users who feel that language and culture cannot be separated without losing the authenticity of the original prefer to read literature and watch English language films in the original, without dubbing or subtitling. The desire for a consistency of theme, language, and culture is one motivation for listening to songs with English lyrics among users with an interest in rock music. A means of access to and direct contact with the local culture when traveling or on vacation in an English-speaking country motivates the use of English, too.

2.5   LEVELS OF PROFICIENCY

As already described in the section on English in the workplace, competence in this language is a common qualification for employment in industry as well as service sectors of Europe. In the former, English is mostly required in fine mechanics, mechanical engineering, vehicle construction, plastics and iron processing, and steel and metal production. In the service sector, employees in the restaurant, hotel, and tourism business, the catering industry, transportation, wholesale and export trades, and banks need high proficiency in English. Elsewhere, adults needing English proficiency range from diplomats to company representatives to taxi drivers. The value placed on English in so many occupations is evident in position announcements in newspapers. Positions that have been advertised in leading German newspapers included those for a journalist with "perfect" English, a mechanical engineer with several years of technical English, a social worker with "good" English, and a manager in a pharmaceuticals firm with "good" knowledge of English. English is also requisite for academic positions in the Netherlands. Increasingly these ads are in English, which follows a trend not only in international newspapers but also in Dutch-language newspapers, for example, *De Volkskrant.*

These few examples of position announcements beg a question highly relevant with respect to English: To what extent are Europeans proficient in English? The European Commission has conducted surveys to determine proficiency in various languages, the results of which are published regularly in its Eurobarometer reports. Keeping in mind that the basis for these reports are self-assessments and that such data cannot be compared with demonstrations of language use in communicative situations, information from various Eurobarometer surveys do shed light on Europeans' perceptions of their ability to use various languages, including English.

In 2001, as reported in Eurobarometer 54.1 (European Commission, 2001b), those surveyed most often claimed English as the language they could communicate in or knew better than other European languages. For European languages in general, 53% said they could speak at least one European language in addition to their mother tongue; 26% said they could speak two foreign languages. English was the language that most (41%) tended to know besides their mother tongue; French was next at 19%, followed by German (10%) and Spanish (7%). The least claimed to know Italian (3%).

A subsequent report found that among Germans 15 years of age and older, 44% claimed to be able to participate in a conversation in English (just 12% claimed to be able to speak French) (European Commission, 2001b). Compared to Eurobarometer surveys from previous years, this figure marks a steady increase in language proficiency: in 1998 it was 41% and in 1990 just 34%. In an earlier national study, Hasebrink (1997) asked adults 18 years and older for self assessments of whether they were able to roughly understand a selection of media types - a newspaper article, TV news, TV movies (without subtitles), or radio programs – in various languages. Over 31% of the respondents responded affirmatively on at least one of the four media for English. There was, however, a clear difference between respondents from western Germany (33.9%) and eastern Germany (21.9%), an outcome possibly influenced by the distinct histories of contact with English for each region.

The Netherlands present yet a different picture. In a (fairly small-scale) study, Janssen, Janssen-van Dieten, & Evers (1997) compared the English language proficiency profiles of Dutch pupils aged 15-16 with peers from France, Spain and Sweden using tests that focused on both receptive and productive grammatical and pragmatic skills. Data showed that Dutch pupils scored 68% correct on the grammatical and 62% on the productive written skills. Overall the score was 67% correct. For the other groups, mean scores correct were 37% (France), 35% (Spain) and 60% (Sweden).

The differences in the scores were only partly explained by differences in contact time in the class: as mentioned above, Dutch pupils receive on average 150 minutes of English teaching per week. French and Spanish pupils' English lessons take 180 minutes per week. Teaching time is still less for Swedish pupils at 120 minutes per week. In all countries, there were significant differences between school types. In the Netherlands, mean correct scores ranged from 46% for the lowest educational level, which prepares pupils for vocational training, 63% for the intermediate level, 76% for the more advanced level, and up to 79% for the pupils preparing for university.

The self-report data included in a 1999 Eurobarometer report showed that 62% of Belgians (age 15 or older and from Flemings and Wallons combined) claimed to be able to carry on a conversation in at least one other foreign language (European Commission, 1999). Forty-one percent claimed to be able to do this in English, 14% in German, and 38% in French, and 3% for Italian and Spanish. Complementary data is found in the anecdotal evidence from Goethals (1997), who has observed that on the whole Belgian travelers abroad, and Flemings in particular, do relatively well at the survival level when speaking to foreigners. English-speaking visitors report no problems when speaking with people on the street or in shops .

In Eurobarometer 50 (European Commission, 1999), it is reported that 45% of the French surveyed claimed to be able to take part in a conversation in a language other than their mother tongue. Thirty two per cent claimed knowledge of English as a "second language". Spanish (11%) and German (9%) were the other most widely spoken languages apart from French. In a previous report (European Commission, 1997), 63.3% of French youth thought they knew English well enough to participate in a conversation in English, and 17.5% said they would like to speak English better if given the opportunity. Thirty-seven percent had visited the UK in the previous two years. By comparison, 24.7% thought they knew Spanish well enough to participate in a conversation and 21.6% said they would like to learn Spanish if they had the opportunity; 30% had visited Spain.

Being proficient in a language has been shown to have a link with attitudes toward that language and its speakers. Perceptions of the ease of learning a language are one dimension of attitude. Oud-de Glas (1997) found in a study of the Netherlands that among the younger generations English is considered the most easily learned foreign language. Even though no linguistic reasons can be cited for this view (because German is likely to be typologically closer than English) pupils appeared to find German more difficult. This preference, Oud-de-Glas suggests, has an attitudinal rather than a linguistic basis because the older generation in their 60s and 70s considered English more difficult than German.

In a Belgian study, Verluyten, Thiré & Demarest (1994) found that among Flemish university students the transition from language learning at the secondary level to university was perceived as being easier for English than for French: thirty per cent found the transition for English difficult and 42% for French. Flemish reaction to the dominance of English in a recent song contest illustrates another dimension of language attitude. With seven of the twelve songs in English, some Flemish listeners asked, "Do we have to become English-speaking, after we've been submitted for years to pressures to become French-speaking?" (p. 10).

2.6   ATTITUDES

According to various published reports in the last decade or so, Europeans overall seem to have a favorable attitude toward languages other than their own and rank English highly as a school subject. The European Commission (1997) found that 72% believed that knowing foreign languages was or would be useful for them, and 93% of parents with children under age 20 said it was important for their children to learn other European languages. Seventy-one per cent said that everyone in the European Union should be able to speak one European language in addition to their mother tongue. Reasons given for foreign language proficiency included an increase in employment opportunities, recognition that a particular language was widely spoken in the world, and parental desire for their children to be multilingual.

In Belgium, at least among young people, the general attitude towards English appears to be positive. In Wallonia, pupils prefer English classes to Dutch classes, because "they are more lively" (Coppieters 't Wallant, 1997). In Flanders, English classes are also more appreciated than French classes; Flemish children are more motivated to learn English than French, and they show a greater feeling of success at learning English (Sercu 2000, p. 204).

In Germany it is difficult to determine the extent and nature of beliefs about the language and its linguistic, cultural, and social impact because empirical studies of attitudes toward English among Germans are few. Yet, the extensive use of English and consumption of English language cultural products could be interpreted as indications of a positive disposition among some segments of the population. The ease with which new phenomena and trends are either given or adopt an English name, which is subsequently used and widely accepted, also suggests a positive attitude (compare French efforts to curb this practice). Examples include new sports activities such as jogging, walking, snowboarding, and inline skating. Today "faxen," "mailen," or "surfen" are usually used for the respective activities. A noteworthy example is "Handy," the English word that names the ubiquitous mobile phone. Those Germans who assume this is the same name used in Britain or the U.S., which it is not, get upset when they discover English native speakers do not understand what they mean when they refer to their "Handy." Another recent example is "Beamer", which is used to refer to what in the US is called a power point projector.

For the Netherlands, as for Germany, there is little empirical evidence on attitudes towards English. Yet, what data there are seem to suggest that English is seen as a useful and attractive language and not a threat to the Dutch language.

Enthusiasm for using or learning English does not, however, imply widespread acceptance and positive attitudes toward the pervasive presence of English. While young people may be less critical, there are adults who –

although they recognize the need for facility in English and even strongly encourage their children to become fluent in it – have concerns about its presence in their language and its expanding role in more areas of their lives. Some fear that in time English could completely replace the native language for future generations or have serious consequences for the integrity of that language. This tension between fear of English influence and the general perception of the necessity of English is not isolated to one country or another, but is common throughout Europe. Still, each country responds individually.

Lack of empirical evidence on Dutch attitudes has not kept various academics from expressing their fear that Dutch will be replaced by English in the near future (e.g., Beheydt, 1996; de Swaan, 1991). These fears are not supported by a pilot study in which 69 immigrants from 31 different countries were questioned about their language attitudes and intentions to learn other languages (Weltens & De Bot, 1995). The main conclusion of the study, which was motivated by impressions in various immigration countries that immigrants "skip" the national language and try to learn a larger international language in order to move on, was that among immigrants in the Netherlands, at any rate, learning English, for all its attractiveness in other respects, is not seen as an alternative to learning Dutch.

The Belgian general public expressed concern about the future of the use of English in higher education as early as the 1990s. This issue is of especially keen interest in Flanders. After a long struggle for the use of Dutch rather than French in higher education, the Flemish decree aimed at protecting the Dutch language now forbids higher education in any language other than Dutch. It states that university programs can only exist in English if they also exist in Dutch. The question here is whether English – along with French –becomes a threat to Dutch.

France has a long tradition of favorable attitudes to English which dates from the 18th century. At the time, even though France and England were fighting fiercely against one another in North America, philosophers looked to Britain for examples of parliamentarian democracy and encyclopedists for new techniques. Unfavorable attitudes are more recent and reached a peak in the 1960s with the publication of René Etiemble's *Parlez-vous franglais?* in 1963. Its subsequent and considerable impact on the image of linguistic resistance to English can be observed in French attempts in the 1970s and 1990s to pass laws that would protect and preserve French from foreignisms, most especially Anglicisms and Americanisms. These efforts have had no lasting success.

Some Germans opposed to the prevalence of English words and the frequency with which they are used by their compatriots have, like their French counterparts, sought to draft a law to protect the language, and urge the government to set the example by using German words to replace now more commonly used English words. Specific examples are the use of

Treffpunkt, not <u>Meeting-Point</u>; <u>Büro,</u> not <u>Office</u>; and <u>Lehrpläne,</u> not <u>Curricula</u> (Lammert, 2001).

2.7 THE FUTURE OF ENGLISH

As is evident in this sociolinguistic profile of English in Europe, English is very present in Europe and its presence is best understood in the context of both the European Union as a whole and of countries and regions in particular. Prominent in the media, in education, in science and technology, and in the workplace, high levels of English proficiency are claimed by learners and desired by employees, and both positive and negative attitudes are held. Germany dubs films, while the Netherlands subtitles; English is used in higher education in the Netherlands more than in France; Belgium has two official state languages, but Germany only one; France attempts to control the influence of English through legislation, while Belgium focuses on the balance between Dutch and French.

The future of English in Europe depends to a large extent upon how its use and learning develops both within individual countries and within succeeding generations. As Graddol (2001), Crystal (1997), and Fishman (1998/1999), among many others have forecast, the place of English, at least for the foreseeable future, is secure. And in Europe, as elsewhere, for better or worse, it will expand within specific domains of use and increase in the number of users. Being the first foreign language in most schools and introduced at school at ever earlier stages, expanded knowledge of and higher proficiency levels in English can be anticipated as well. Similarly, its extensive use in higher education from lecture halls to libraries in response to internationalization, and the need to compete with other European institutions for the revenue that international students bring, will be additional factors in its future.

It also must be noted that the future of English is closely tied to the other languages of Europe, which begs an intriguing question: What will the kind and nature of the interplay between these languages and English be in this internationalized scenario? An example is German's position as a language of wider communication in Eastern Europe, where German, as a linguistic artifact of the Austro-Hungarian Empire, has been taught and used throughout the 20th century, even during the Soviet era. Thus, the use of English for wider communication is limited. Yet, this may change depending to some extent upon patterns of English learning and use with the admission of the Czech Republic, Estonia, Hungary, Latvia, Lithuania, Poland, Slovakia, Slovenia (along with Malta) to the EU. Current political strategies in Germany could also help to tip the balance. Strategies designed to enhance the position of Germany in the areas of science and business explicitly specify that English proficiency should be improved on all levels.

This composite sociolinguistic profile of English in Belgium, France, Germany, and the Netherlands has outlined the role of school, social background, attitudes, and contact with English, through the media in particular. But data is lacking that allows comprehensive comparison between countries, and in most countries even basic data on any one of these roles are missing. Thus, we used the roles of school, social background, attitudes and contact as a starting point for the design of the survey questionnaire and for an analysis of the findings.

In order to measure the differential impact of those factors the same set of data had to be gathered in different countries and the effect they have on language proficiency, which is ultimately the most important aspect from a language policy perspective, needed to be assessed. The next chapter describes the components and characteristics of the study of the presence of English in Europe, media, and European youth that we undertook to make up for data that has been lacking.

Chapter 3

AN EMPIRICAL APPROACH TO THE PRESENCE OF ENGLISH

Margie Berns

3.1   INTRODUCTION

The sociolinguistic profile presented in Chapter 2 provided a broad, panoramic view of English in Europe to serve as the backdrop and contextualization for the issues we explored in our study. Insight into the sociolinguistics of English as well as other languages in which the young people we surveyed find themselves is a keystone in the foundation that supports our goals. The lack of empirical data on one aspect or other of the presence of English in the four countries was noted in the profile as well. As a first step toward filling these gaps, we designed a systematic investigation of the presence of English across Europe and among European youth in particular.

3.2   FOCUS ON YOUTH

A key player in the process of globalization – both in acting upon and reacting to it – is the younger generation. The effects of globalization, the impact of the formation of an international information society, and the myriad issues facing the "new" Europe are interrelated matters that today's young Europeans will have to grapple with as they carry on the building of an increasingly interconnected and unified Europe. As the most information technology literate segment of the population, the most conversant in inter- and cross-cultural communication, and among the most catered to group by the services and programs of the European Union, the youth of Europe make an obvious choice as the focus of our investigation.

Specifically, as they are the ultimate beneficiaries of EU sponsored initiatives geared toward improved and expanded language teaching in primary and secondary education we felt confident that some insight could be gained into both their present and (near) future sociolinguistic situation vis-à-vis the learning and use of English and of media in which contact with English is a feature. Further, it is not insignificant that English is often identified as playing a role in the global youth culture.

Admittedly, the issues we chose to address in this investigation are broad. Any research project of international scope that sets out to explore these issues presents considerable practical and organizational challenges. We acknowledged potential obstacles and recognized that whatever type of study we would design and implement would represent a first small step of many and could only begin to scratch the surface of the complexity and sheer magnitude of issues related to the forces of globalization, the impact of the internet, and the creation of a "new Europe."

3.3   BASIC ASSUMPTIONS AND RESEARCH QUESTIONS

Basic assumptions guiding the design and implementation of the study, as identified in Chapter 1, were the following: (1) different types and levels of English proficiency are attained in different contexts (as suggested by comparison across the four country profiles); (2) descriptions of communicative competence depend on what users can do with a language, rather than their knowledge about the language alone; (3) media, in particular those featuring English, relate to functional language proficiency (or communicative competence); (4) amount and type of exposure to English, in general, has some relationship to attitudes toward English as well as its speakers; and, (5) that attitudes toward both English and English-speaking cultures differ according to people's attitudes toward European languages and their respective cultures. These assumptions provided the structure for identification of four areas of inquiry: (1) the role of schooling in learning of English; (2) the media and other opportunities for contact with English outside school; (3) learner motivation and attitudes toward English; and (4) competence in English.

The specific research questions that these areas addressed were the following:

1.   *Family background* – How does the home environment impact young people's access to media? What impact do parents' levels of education have on young people's attitudes toward English? On opportunities for travel to places where use of English is necessary? Or for use of English outside school and the family?

2.   *Contact with English* - Where do young people have contact with English? How frequently is English used, in what situations,

and with whom? Is English used through oral interaction, written interaction, or both?

    3. *Language attitudes* - What impact has English language media on motivation for learning and using as well as attitudes toward English? What is the relationship between the use of English and attitudes toward it?

    4. *English proficiency* - What is the impact of English language media on the acquisition of English? What is the influence of exposure to and use of English via media on vocabulary development? What are the effects of the media on the development of a functional proficiency in English? What is the role of English language media in developing the communicative competence appropriate for EU uses and users of English?

Our findings, we believed, would be of potential value to researchers, scholars, and practitioners in such fields as first and second language pedagogy and acquisition; language policy and planning; communication and media; sociolinguistics; and, educational and social psychology. Findings on the relationship of media use to language proficiency, for example, could have significance for the ways schools react to and take advantage of media influences on English acquisition and implement new information technologies in teaching (e-mail, web searches, interactive video, or audio streaming). Also of interest were implications of the future role of media and information technologies for young people and their relationship to the so-called information society they will live in. Yet other findings could have implications for ways of approaching language policy and planning issues relating to the present and future role of English in the EU, for example, concerns about the presence and prevalence of English in the media both as a threat to the notion of a European identity and as a contributing factor in the creation of such an identity.

3.4   METHOD

We felt we could best gather this information by means of a school-based survey of youth in the four countries. This method would allow us to get data from a large number of young people quickly and efficiently in a variety of educational, linguistic, and social contexts. We used two data collection approaches: a survey questionnaire and assessment of language proficiency.

3.4.1 Survey questionnaire

We created a survey questionnaire (See Appendix A) that differentiated four parallel areas of daily life - family background, contact with English, language attitudes, and English proficiency – and addressed various aspects of each. Using rating and categorical scales, the questionnaire solicited information about the following:

> 1. General background information (e.g., school, age, sex, place of birth, language used in the home, proficiency of family members).
>
> 2. Language contact at school (e.g., amount of instruction, time spent on homework, use of English in the classroom) and outside school (e.g., at home, via media, friends, and visits abroad).
>
> 3. Language attitudes (e.g., toward English and, in the German sample, other languages).
>
> 4. Language proficiency (e.g., last school grade for English and scales for a global self-assessment of the traditional four skill areas).

Two versions of the questionnaire were used. An evaluation of the items used in the first administration in the Netherlands determined that the questionnaire as administered was too long and that it solicited information not easily scored and interpreted or that did not directly address the main focus of the study. Consequently, the questionnaire was changed: items were deleted, split into subparts, or re-formatted. Version 1 asked respondents to indicate total frequency of TV viewing, regardless of network or station; Version 2 had a frequency scale for each network or station viewed. Version 1 asked a series of specific questions about school use and contact with English. In Version 2, the only item related to school was the assessment of the portion of their knowledge of English they had acquired via school in addition to media and any other sources of contact. Consequently, the removed items were not included in the analyses reported on in following chapters.

Both versions included a set of core items, which had been written in English and then translated into German, French, and Dutch. Although we used two versions, the differences between them are refinements and the overall overlap is sufficient for the analyses to include data from both.

Particular interests of research team members also introduced differences. The administration in Liège asked teachers to assess each pupil's proficiency in reading, speaking, listening and writing in the same global form as their pupils were asked. German members of the team were interested in comparison of respondents' attitudes toward Germany and Germans with those toward other countries; their surveys inquired after attitudes toward France, the Netherlands, Turkey, the U.S., the U.K. and their respective languages. In the Dutch administration, 13 questions about functional proficiency were added to those already in the German pilot study version, as were 10 on speaking and 11 on listening. These items were also used in Flanders, that is, the items were the same for all the pupils who completed the first version of the questionnaire.

3.4.2 "Can do" Scales and vocabulary test

Language proficiency was determined using three measures:

      1.   Global self-assessment of proficiency in each of the four traditional skill areas (reading, writing, speaking, and listening) were inserted into the questionnaire for rating on a 4-point scale (exception: a seven point scale for Liège).

      2.   Self-assessment of functional proficiency in a variety of specific language use situations on a four point scale.

      3.   A vocabulary test.

Each measure served a distinct purpose. The global self-assessments in the traditional skill areas were included to get converging evidence on language proficiency. Of interest were the comparison of relations between the two self-assessment instruments and the vocabulary test.

Although self-assessment scales are regularly criticized for lack of validity, we chose to use them as a measure of respondents' perceptions of their English proficiency for two reasons: they would be less imposing on the amount of time we could ask of classroom teachers, and the lack of the availability of a generally accepted standardized test of English language proficiency for school-age learners. The items used for the "can do" scale were partly taken from Clark & Jorden (1984) and adopted from Grendel (1993) (see Appendix B). More importantly, a standardized test of knowledge of English would not address our concerns with the functional proficiency of the teenagers in our study.

The vocabulary test (Meara, 1992; Meara & Jones, 1988; 1990; see Appendix B) was used for two primary reasons. The first was prior experience with the test that had assessed its validity (see Huibregste, 2001). The second is ease of administration and scoring. The test has good psychometric properties that made us confident in its appropriateness for the study, and it is wide ranging yet sensitive to small differences (see Meara & Buxton, 1987). A further reason to use this test was its correlation with proficiency in the four so-called skill areas (speaking, listening, reading, and writing). Meara (1992) has made claims for this correlation, and Huibregtse, Admiraal & Meara, (2002) have found a correlation with reading and oral proficiency measures.

The test has a simple format. Respondents are presented with a set of items. Using a yes/no format, respondents are asked to distinguish real words from pseudo-words; two thirds were real words and one third was pseudo-words. The pseudo-words are letter strings that meet the phonotactic constraints of the language but have no meaning (e.g., *baptistal, immagical*). Using a combination of "hits" and "false alarms" based on signal detection theory, it's possible to establish a measure of the knowledge of words in a given frequency range and to correct for guessing. The paper-and-pencil version of the test has 10 parallel tests for 5 frequency ranges: >1000, >2000, >3000, >4000, and >5000. A score of 45, for example, means the respondent has knowledge of 45% of the words in that range.

The test also comes in different lengths, an important consideration when time available for administration varies from site to site. The 120-item version was used in Germany, Flanders, and the Netherlands; the 60-item version was administered in Walloon schools. On both, two thirds of the words were bona fide English words and one third pseudo-words.

3.4.3   Participants

Between 1995 and 2000, a total of 2,248 school pupils completed the questionnaires and the vocabulary test in six separate cross-sectional administrations: two in the Netherlands (one group attending monolingual schools and one group attending Dutch/English bilingual schools), two in Belgium (one group Dutch-speaking and the other French-speaking), one in Germany, and one in France. Part of the participants in the Dutch monolingual group and Dutch bilingual group completed the first version of the questionnaire (221 out of 800 and 55 out of 328, respectively), as did the total Dutch-speaking Brussels group. All other participants completed the second version.

The participants attended a variety of school types in Belgium (Liège and Brussels), France (Valence), Germany (Hamburg), and cities and small towns in the Netherlands. School types ranged from general education to university preparatory, both monolingual and bilingual schools. It is necessary to point out here that the groups are not completely equivalent because of differences in the ages of pupils at each level and the focus of education or training at each level. Due to this lack of comparability we do not claim that our findings can be generalized to other groups in the countries involved.

Tables 3.1-3.4 show the breakdown of participants by school type and by country.

Table 3.1
Number of subjects from each school type – Belgium

School type	Participants
Secondary school – Wallonia	118
Secondary school – Flanders	208
Total	326

Table 3.2
Number of subjects from each school type – France

School type	Participants
Vocational high school, Valence	147
Total	147

Table 3.3
Number of subjects from each school type – Germany

School type	Participants
Grammar school	335
Secondary school	172
Extended elementary school	140
Total	647

Table 3.4
Number of subjects from each school type – Netherlands

School type	Participants
Basic general secondary (mavo)	73
Pre-vocational secondary (havo)	175
College preparatory secondary (vwo)	353
Pre-class basic/vocational secondary (mavo/havo)	44
Pre-class vocational/college preparatory secondary (havo/vwo)	155
Bilingual college preparatory secondary	328
Total	1128

The young people who participated in the study ranged in age from 12 – 18 (mean of 15) and consisted of more girls (51.6%) than boys (47.8%). (See Appendix C, Table C1, and D, Table D2 for age and sex breakdown by groups.). Most (91.3%) were born in the country in which the research was done. While most of those born in a country other than the research country have a migrant background, some of those born in a research country also may have such a background (see Table 3.5).

In the presence of English

Table 3.5
Country of birth by research group in percentages of the number of students from whom data are available (N)

Country of birth	Netherlands		Netherlands (bilingual school)		Flanders		Wallonia		Germany		France		Total sample	
	N	%	N	%	N	%	N	%	N	%	N	%	N	%
Research country	739	96.3	285	88.0	193	97.5	113	95.8	518	82.9	139	96.5	1987	91.3
Europe, English speaking	2	.3	1	.3					1	.2			4	.2
rest Europe	13	1.7	10	3.1	2	1.0	3	2.5	70	11.2			98	4.5
non-Europe, English speaking	2	.3	6	1.9	1	.5			4	.6	1	.7	14	.6
rest non-Europe	11	1.4	22	6.8	2	1.0	2	1.7	32	5.1	4	2.8	73	3.4
Total	767	100.0	324	100.0	198	100.0	118	100.0	625	100.0	144	100.0	2176	100.0

Research groups

The proportion of those born outside of the research country is low, except for the German group at 17% and the Dutch bilingual school group with 12%. An explanation for the German figures is that the data was gathered in a large city where higher percentages would be expected. The Dutch bilingual groups percentage can be explained by their enrollment in college preparatory schools located in smaller cities. It is also worth noting that the parents of the non-Dutch born students are generally highly educated (see Chapter 4) and may find the bilingual school form especially attractive. It does have to be kept in mind that not all the students born outside the four research countries necessarily have a migrant background, or that those with such background could have been born in the research country.

All attended schools in urban settings. Urban settings were selected because of the size and diversity of their population, availability and access to the widest range of media offerings, and schools in these locales are most likely to be equipped with the latest technologies. Convenience sampling was the basis for selection of the particular schools. Where required, permission to conduct the study was secured from school authorities and permission for the children to participate was sought from parents and guardians as well as declarations of willingness to be a participant from the children themselves. In Germany we were obligated to follow strict protocols for permission to gather personal data. Surveys were either sent to the school for distribution by the classroom teacher or were administered to intact classes during regular school hours under the direct supervision of a research team member or associate. The full class period was devoted to completion of the questionnaire and vocabulary test.

3.4.4 Analyses

As a first step, the full breadth of the data was examined in a descriptive way, breaking down all relevant variables for the six cross-sectional groups (Chapter 4). In the second step, the large number of variables was reduced to four small sets of indicator variables for the areas "Contact," "Attitudes," "Proficiency," and "Family background." By means of analysis of variance, similarities and differences between groups were identified, and using path-analyses the causal relations between the four sets of variables were investigated (Chapter 5). The third step in the analysis was an examination of the patterns of media use with respect to different analytical perspectives (Chapter 6).

Chapter 4

DESCRIPTIVE FINDINGS ON THE PRESENCE OF ENGLISH

Kees de Bot, Riet Evers, and Ineke Huibregtse

4.1   INTRODUCTION

The focus of this chapter is the presentation of descriptive findings and comparative data, which are organized into four headings. Each category characterizes a conceptual dimension of our study: (1) school; (2) media and other sources of contact with English; (3) attitudes towards English; and, (4) English language proficiency. A more focused and refined analysis of these data will be reported in Chapter 5, where the aim is to identify possible relationships between and among the four sets of data.

4.2   FAMILY CHARACTERISTICS

The heading "Family characteristics" covers the outcomes of the questions related to family background. The data included in it are: (1) the educational level of the pupils' parents; (2) the language(s) spoken at home; and, (3) pupils' assessments of their parents' and siblings' level of English language proficiency. Missing from this analysis are the items "occupation of the father" and "occupation of the mother". These were dropped because the occupation names given by the pupils were often so vague and ambiguous that a classification was not feasible.

4.2.1   Educational level of the parents

As pointed out in Chapters 2 and 3, school types differ across the four countries included in the survey. These differences make any direct cross-country comparison of school types nearly impossible. However, because learning as much as we could about the role of educational background was an objective, we needed some way to make a distinction among the school types. Our solution was to distinguish between three rather broad levels of education for each country, which can be globally described as low, medium, and high. In Table 4.1 the highest level of education attained by parents (at least one) is presented.

Table 4.1
Highest level of education of either parent by research group in percentages of the number of students from whom data are available (N)

				Level of education		
		N	A	B	C	Total
Research groups	Nn	733	26.3	50.4	23.3	100.0
	Nb	226	11.5	32.3	56.2	100.0
	Bd	195	19.0	25.6	55.4	100.0
	Bf	118	11.9	20.3	67.8	100.0
	G	553	51.9	21.5	26.6	100.0
	F	140	35.7	45.7	18.6	100.0

[1]A = primary /secondary education; B = higher vocational training; C = university
[2]A = primary/lower secondary education; B = Gymnasium/Abitur; C = university

As the table indicates, for the Dutch (hereafter Nn = normal education group and Nb = bilingual education group) especially, parents of those in bilingual schools have a fairly high level of education. That is, the 26% in the Nn group had at least one parent with an education at the primary/secondary level. More than 50% of the children have at least one parent with a university degree. The Belgian (hereafter Bd = Dutch speaking Belgians and Bf =French speaking Belgians) pupils also report high levels of education. The highest level of education for most parents in the French group (hereafter F) is the intermediate level, while the majority of the German (hereafter G) groups report a lower level of education (primary or lower secondary education). We have to note here that a fairly large number provided no information on parents' level of education.

We want to note that, in order to make the presentation of the data more concise and insightful, scale data have been treated as interval data in the description and analysis. We are aware that this is problematic from a strict statistical point of view, but an adherence to scale data would have made accessible presentation of the multitude of data virtually impossible,

4.2.2   Home languages

Responses to the three items on language or languages spoken at home (one item each on father's mother tongue, mother's mother tongue, and andlanguage child uses at home) allow for a rather broad interpretation: if the parents have English-speaking friends who come to visit regularly, the student may indicate that (sometimes) English is spoken at home. Various combinations of languages that the children speak at home are shown in Table 4.2.

Table 4.2
Languages spoken at home by students in percentages of the number of students from whom data are available (N)

	Research groups						Total sample
Home languages	Nn (N=766)	Nb (N=325)	Bd (N=199)	Bf (N=118)	G (N=633)	F (N=145)	(N=2186)
only national	91.5	79.4	100.0	87.3	74.9	91.0	85.4
only English	0.1	0.6					.1
English + other					0.5	0.7	.2
national + English (+ other)	2.2	13.8			0.8	1.4	3.2
national + other	4.0	3.4		11.9	14.4	6.2	7.1
only other	2.1	2.8		0.8	9.5	0.7	4.0
Total	100.0	100.0	100.0	100.0	100.0	100.0	100.0

Most students appear to speak only one language at home, and it is mostly the national language. A few of these results merit closer consideration. In Germany, 9.5% speak a language other than either the national language or English at home. Interestingly, for this group the "only other" score was 29.8% for the fathers and 28.4% for the mothers. The 14.4% of the students for "national + other" suggests that the national language is used at home even though quite a few parents use only another language.

The situation is different for the Dutch bilingual group. Here 13.8% report the use of the national language plus English. As only 7 out of 324 students in this group were born in an English speaking country, the figure for the use of English probably in part reflects broad interpretation of the question asked.

4.2.3   English proficiency of parents and siblings

The students were asked to indicate on a 7-point scale (from *not at all* to *very good*) how well their parents and their siblings knew English. Table 4.3 shows the mean levels of proficiency for parents (average of the combined scores of the father and mother) and for siblings (children under the age of 5 were not taken into account). The descriptors for the scores are 1(*not at all*); 2 (*very bad*); 3 (*bad*); 4 (*rather good*); 5 (*good*); and, 6 (*very good*).

Table 4.3
Estimated levels of English language proficiency of parents and siblings,
with the mean, the standard deviation (s.d.) and the number of students on
which the means are based (N)

		English language proficiency of parents			English language proficiency of siblings (age>4)		
		Mean	s.d.	N	mean	s.d.	N
Research groups	Nn	5.2	1.1	796	4.7	1.5	738
	Nb	5.5	1.1	325	4.7	1.7	295
	Bd	5.2	1.0	208	5.0	1.2	192
	Bf	3.8	1.6	117	3.6	1.9	104
	G	4.2	1.7	618	4.5	1.6	497
	F	3.0	1.4	145	4.0	1.6	128
Total sample		4.7	1.5	2209	4.6	1.6	1954

The estimated mean level of the parents for all of the Dutch speaking groups lies between, *rather good* and *good*; for the French group the mean was 3, or *bad*. The German- and French-speaking Belgian parents fall in between. The means of proficiency among siblings yield a slightly different picture. Here the division seems to be between speakers of Dutch and speakers of French, with speakers of German in between. For almost all groups, the mean score for the siblings lies somewhat below the mean score of the parents; the only exception is the French group, where the siblings score is a full point higher than the mean score of the parents (i.e., *rather bad* vs. *bad*).

4.3   CONTACT WITH ENGLISH: OPPORTUNITIES

In the first version of the questionnaire, 13 different opportunities for contact with English were presented. In the second version the item "school" was, for nearly all groups, deleted and replaced by the item "traveling abroad". The only exception is the questionnaire used for the German group, in which both items were presented. Students were asked to indicate on a four-point scale (1 *for never* to 4, *very often*) how often they were in contact with English through the people and media listed. The outcomes are presented in Table 4.4.

Table 4.4

Contact with English by research group, with the mean (m), the standard deviation (s.d.) and the number of students on which the means are based (N)

| | | | | | | | Research groups | | | | | | | | |
| Opportunity | Nn (N=739) | | Nb (N=265) | | Bd (N=190) | | Bf (N=110) | | G (N=593) | | F (N=129) | | Total sample (N=2026) | |
	m	s.d.	m	s.d.	m	s.d.	m	s.d.	m	s.d.	m	s.d.	m	s.d.
parents	1.8	.8	2.0	.9	1.6	.6	1.6	.7	1.5	.6	1.4	.6	1.7	.7
siblings	1.7	.7	1.8	.9	1.5	.7	1.5	.7	1.6	.7	1.5	.6	1.6	.7
Friends	1.9	.7	2.4	.9	1.9	.7	2.1	.8	1.9	.7	1.6	.6	2.0	.8
Radio music	3.4	.8	3.4	.8	3.5	.7	3.3	.8	3.5	.8	3.0	.9	3.4	.8
speech on radio	1.9	.8	1.8	.8	1.8	.8	1.2	.4	2.4	1.1	1.9	1.0	2.0	.9
TV	3.4	.7	3.6	.6	3.3	.8	2.5	.9	2.5	.9	1.9	.8	3.0	.9
CD/cassettes	3.5	.7	3.6	.6	3.7	.6	3.4	.8	3.6	.7	3.1	.9	3.5	.7
cinema	3.1	1.0	3.4	.9	3.2	.9	2.2	.9	2.0	.8	1.7	.7	2.7	1.1
papers	1.4	.6	1.6	.7	1.3	.6	1.4	.6	1.8	.8	1.2	.5	1.5	.7
magazines	1.8	.7	2.2	.8	1.7	.8	1.9	.8	2.0	.8	1.5	.6	1.9	.8
Books	1.9	.8	2.9	.8	2.0	.6	1.8	.8	1.6	.7	1.2	.5	1.9	.8
computers	2.9	1.0	3.2	.9	2.5	.9	2.9	1.0	3.0	1.0	2.1	1.0	2.9	1.0
traveling abroad*	2.6	1.0	2.9	.9			2.4	1.0	2.6	1.1	1.9	.9	2.6	1.0
teacher**	3.5	.7			3.4	.7			3.6	.6			3.5	.7

* for the Nn group N=539, for the total sample N=1636

** for the Nn group N=200, for the total sample N=983

The main opportunities for contact with English are via radio music, CD's and cassettes, TV, the English teacher at school, and, to a lesser extent, computers and traveling abroad.

An interesting difference between the Dutch speaking groups (Nn, Nb, and Bd) and the other groups regards the results for TV and cinema. The Dutch speaking students have a mean of > 3.0, while the other groups have a score of < 3.0 (*often*). It is useful to recall here that foreign programs and films in the Netherlands and in Flanders are subtitled, while in French- and German-speaking countries they are dubbed. The findings suggests that TV and cinema offer different opportunities for contact with English for the different groups.

We also looked at groups of items. Of note is that, though the mean scores on the individual items "parents", "siblings" and "friends" are rather low for all research groups, in the Dutch bilingual schools (Nb) 94.8% indicate at least one of these categories as a source of contact with English. For all other groups the figures are considerably lower. The same is true for contact through newspapers, magazines, and books. In this case, the Dutch bilingual group had only 0.6% indicating no contact with English via these print media, while it was 46.9% for the French group.

4.3.1   Listening to music

With respect to music, students were asked to indicate how many hours a week they listen to music, the language of the songs they listen to, and how important they find the lyrics of the music they listen to in relation to the language of the lyrics. The data in Table 4.5 show that the G group spends about 28 hours a week listening to music. For the other groups the figures are somewhat lower, but still close to two hours a day or more. Data of the Bd group are not given here due to errors that occurred in survey administration.

Table 4.5
Reported duration of listening to music in hours per week,
with the mean, the standard deviation (s.d.) and the number
of students who answered the question (N)

		Number of hours per week		
		mean	s.d.	N
Research groups	Nn	18.6	17.5	779
	Nb	18.8	15.1	320
	Bd	-	-	-
	Bf	13.3	12.9	117
	G	28.1	19.0	621
	F	14.3	14.0	143
Total sample		21.0	17.9	1983

Quite revealing are the data on the language of song lyrics and the importance attached to the lyrics in relation to the language they are in (Table 4.6). Large proportions of the Dutch-speaking groups report listening predominantly to English language music. In the other groups English also appears to have a rather strong position. The difference between Bf and F shows that the Bf group listens more to English language music than the participants in France. The majority of the French group listens to both languages, while the Bf group seems to be somewhere between the Dutch speaking and French group. The French-speaking students attach more importance to lyrics of songs in their national language than do the other groups. The groups with the highest proportion of students showing interest in English texts are Bd, Bf, and Nb. All these students are in schools of higher level secondary education. A number of explanations for this are possible. One is that students at higher levels of education may be more interested in lyrics anyway. Another is that their parents, who also have higher levels of education, may encourage them to listen to lyrics. In all groups, texts in other languages are not considered very important. The general tendency is that students listen to English songs a lot, and attach some importance to their lyrics. As a source of English input, the quantity of input is considerable.

Table 4.6
The language of the lyrics the students listen to and the importance they attach to the lyrics in percentages of the number of students per research group who answered the question (N)

| | Research groups | | | | | | Total |
	Nn	Nb	Bd	Bf	G	F	sample
Language of music							
only or mainly national	1.0	0.9	0.5	5.9	2.4	5.0	1.9
only or mainly English	82.4	89.5	89.4	45.8	58.3	24.1	71.5
(about) equally	16.5	9.5	10.1	48.3	39.4	70.9	26.6
N	(792)	(325)	(208)	(118)	(635)	(141)	(2219)
Importance of lyrics in English							
(rather) unimportant	54.1	38.7	34.1	44.4	50.4	60.7	48.9
(rather) important	45.9	61.3	65.9	55.6	49.6	39.3	51.1
N	(796)	(326)	(208)	(117)	(635)	(145)	(2227)
Importance of lyrics in national language							
(rather) unimportant	52.5	46.2	32.2	21.2	38.3	17.4	41.7
(rather) important	47.5	53.8	67.8	78.8	61.7	82.6	58.3
N	(783)	(325)	(199)	(118)	(621)	(144)	(2190)
Importance of lyrics in other languages							
(rather) unimportant	88.2	86.3		72.4	80.7	77.8	83.6
(rather) important	11.8	13.7		27.6	19.3	22.2	16.4
N	(569)	(271)		(116)	(451)	(144)	(1551)

4.3.2   Watching TV and listening to radio

In Table 4.7 the percentages of the research groups are presented who reported watching English language television programs and also the percentages of the groups who claimed to listen to English radio programs.

Table 4.7
Contact with English through watching TV and listening to radio: number of students answering "yes" in percentages of the total number of students per research group from whom data are available (N)

	Research groups						Total sample
	Nn	Nb	Bd	Bf	G	F	
Watching English TV programs							
% yes	90.5	97.9	80.7	77.1	43.7	23.6	72.2
N (=100%)	(798)	(328)	(207)	(118)	(639)	(144)	(2234)
Listening to English radio programs							
% yes	15.4	18.0	16.4	7.6	6.9	6.9	12.5
N (=100%)	(797)	(328)	(207)	(118)	(642)	(145)	(2237)

In all groups the proportion of students claiming to watch English language TV programs appears to be much greater than the proportion that claims to listen to English language radio programs. Regarding TV, the considerable difference in the percentages of students claiming to watch English language TV programs between the German and French groups, on the one hand, and the Dutch and Belgian groups, on the other, can be explained by the different national network policies on the broadcasting of English language programs: Dutch and Belgian networks often subtitle rather than dub English language programs, thereby offering students in these countries more opportunities for contact with English through TV.

Of those who claim to listen to English radio programs, a majority do so less than once a week, except the German group. In it, 54.3% claim to be doing so more than once a week. The cause of this higher than expected figure is unclear to us. It may be the result of how the question was interpreted. It is possible that music radio programs, for example, the locally produced Enjoy and Jam FM that the German groups listed, are seen as English language programs because they play a lot of English language recordings.

The students who indicated that they do watch English language TV programs were asked to answer two further questions: "On which networks do you watch English language programs?" and, "How often do you watch English language programs on each network?" For the data in Table 4.8 we divided the networks listed by the students into two categories: networks which broadcast only English language programs (e.g., BBC, CNN) and, other language networks broadcasting some programs in English (e.g., documentaries, films, soap operas). Networks most frequently listed by

French students claiming to watch English language programs on non-English language networks are La Cinq and Arte (a French/German cultural network).

Looking at the information provided in Table 4.8 on the total frequency of viewing English language programs and type of network viewed (English language/non-English language), we see that the majority of the students indicating they watch English language TV programs claim to do so at least once a week (about 90% for the Dutch groups, about 80% for the German group, about 70% for the Belgian groups, and about 50% for the French group).

Table 4.8
Frequency of watching English language TV programs and types of networks watched by research group in percentages of the number of students from whom data are available (N)

Watching English language TV programs	Research groups						Total sample
	Nn	Nb	Bd	Bf	G	F	
Frequency of watching							
never	9.9	2.2	20.5	23.5	57.8	76.9	28.6
< once a month	2.0	3.4	6.2	8.7	3.4	2.8	3.4
1-3 times a month	7.7	8.4	15.4	10.4	5.1	8.4	7.9
Once a week	16.3	32.3	21.5	10.4	6.7	1.4	15.1
> once a week	64.2	53.7	36.4	47.0	27.0	10.5	45.0
N	(768)	(322)	(195)	(115)	(623)	(143)	(2166)
Type of networks							
only Eng. lang. networks	32.4	28.6	91.6	25.0	84.8	45.5	46.3
Eng lang. networks+other	32.4	56.8	3.9	51.1	11.4	33.3	32.0
Only other networks	35.3	14.6	4.5	23.9	3.8	21.2	21.7
N	(692)	(315)	(155)	(88)	(263)	(33)	(1546)

Nn = normal education; Nb = bilingual education; Bd = Dutch speaking Belgian;
Bf = French speaking Belgian; F = French; G = German

There are salient differences between the two Dutch and the two Belgian groups. About 65% of those in the Dutch normal group watch programs at least partly on English language networks versus about 85% in the Dutch bilingual group (Nb). For the Dutch speaking Belgians (Bd), the percentage was 45.6% versus 60% for the French speaking Belgians (Bf). Parallel to these differences in frequency of watching, the data also suggest differences in watching behavior: the percentage of students never watching programs on English language networks is lower for the Nb and Bd groups than for the Nn and Bf groups, whereas the percentage of students never watching English language programs on non-English language networks is much higher for the Nb and Bd groups than for the other two. Though many students in the Bf group listed both types of networks, Table 4.8 shows that they watch programs on English language networks more frequently. In the German group, too, the students watching English language programs mainly did so on English language networks. For the French group the data suggest a somewhat more varied behavior.

4.3.3   Going on vacation

The survey item soliciting information about contact with English during vacations is not only inquiring about visits to English-speaking countries, but also about the use of English during vacations in any country. The second dimension of the question was to help us find out to what extent these teenagers were using English in encounters with others from different language backgrounds. The percentage of students per group answering "yes" to the question, "Have you ever been on vacation in a country where you've had to use English to make yourself understood?" are presented in Table 4.9.

Table 4.9
Contact with English during holidays by research group: number of students answering
"yes" in percentage of the total number of students from whom data are available (N)

	Research groups						Total sample
	Nn	Nb	Bd	Bf	G	F	(N=2236)
	(N=794)	(N=326)	(N=207)	N=118)	(N=644)	(N=146)	
Use of English during holidays	67.1	89.3	70.5	64.4	66.8	44.2	68.9

We found that, apart from the French group, 66% or more use English during vacations. To get a clearer picture of what these figures might mean, we combined these findings with information about the particular countries visited, which were listed by the students who claimed to have used English on vacations. The countries mentioned were classified into two categories: English speaking and non-English speaking, with the results presented in Table 4.10. Note that the percentages per group do not add up to 100, since many students claimed to have used English in both an English speaking country and a non-English speaking country.

Table 4.10
Classes of countries visited on holiday by research group in percentages of the number of
students from whom data are available (N)

Type of country	Research groups						Total sample
	Nn	Nb	Bd	Bf	G	F	(=1530)
	(N=527)	(N=290)	(N=146)	(N=75)	(N=427)	(N=65)	
English speaking	45.7	83.8	84.2	82.7	51.5	89.2	61.9
non-English speaking	77.4	69.0	41.1	42.7	74.2	29.2	67.7

For four of the six groups, the percentage of students in the first category appears to be (much) higher than the percentage in the second category, yet the data in Table 4.10 clearly show that in all groups a substantial proportion of students, varying from 29.2% in the F group to 77.4% in the Nn group, uses English while on vacation in non-English-speaking countries. English thus appears to be important for teenagers from different European countries as a means of mutual understanding.

4.3.4 Living abroad

Only in the second version of the survey questionnaire were students asked if they had ever lived for a time in a country where they had to use English as a second language. As a result, data on this item are not available for 484 students, including all in the Bd group. Of the 1,764 we do have data on, just 70 (4%) indicated having used English while living abroad. Most of these students, namely 45, belong to the Nb group, with the United Kingdom and the USA as the countries most often given. For this group, the duration of their stay abroad ranged from 1 to 15 years (mean 5.7 years). For those in the other groups who had lived abroad for some time, the time spent ranged from 2 months to 13 years, with a mean of 3.1 years for the Nn group; 0.3 years for the Bf group; 3.4 years for the G group; and 1.0 year for the F group.

4.3.5 English in primary education

There are clear differences between the groups in the percentages of pupils who have had English in primary school: 94.8% for the Nn group; 89.6% for the Nb group; 23.7% for the Bf group; and 28.8% for the F group. (No data is available for the German and Bd groups because none of these students had had English in primary school.) The difference between the two Dutch groups can probably be explained by the Dutch bilingual group's experiences living abroad and attending primary school in another country. While all the pupils in the Nn group should have had English since it is compulsory in Dutch primary education, some 5% have not had English at the primary school level due to such factors as a lack of qualified teachers.

4.3.6 Attitudes toward English

Attitudes towards English were probed through three questions: one on its likeability, one on its importance, and the other through identification of potential advantages for knowing and using English. For all three questions 4-point scales were used. For likeability of English the alternatives ranged from 1 (*I don't like it at all*) to 4 (*I like it very much*), and for its importance from 1 (*not important at all*) to 4 (*very important*). The mean scores on these two questions are presented in Table 4.11. With only one mean slightly below 3 (*more like than dislike* and *rather important*, respectively), the data clearly show that all groups like English and think it is important.

Table 4.11
Likeability and importance of English as reported by the students with the
mean, the standard deviation (s.d.) and the number of students who
answered the question(N)

		Likeability of English			Importance of English		
		mean	s.d.	N	mean	s.d.	N
Research groups	Nn	3.2	.7	791	3.4	.7	795
	Nb	3.5	.5	328	3.7	.5	328
	Bd	3.4	.6	207	3.8	.5	208
	Bf	3.5	.6	118	3.6	.5	118
	G	3.1	.9	640	3.7	.6	642
	F	2.8	.8	147	3.2	.7	146
Total sample		3.2	.7	2231	3.5	.6	2237

To assess perceptions about the advantages of knowing English, a 4-point scale was used to rate degrees of agreement and disagreement with a given set of items. The alternatives ranged from 1 (*I don't agree at all*) to 4 (*I agree completely*). Table 4.12 shows the mean scores on the items. Slight differences in the form of the survey administered for the Bd group account for the empty cells. The last two items were not inserted in the first version of the questionnaire. Since the whole Bd group filled in the first version, there are no data on these two items available for the group.

Communication abroad, comprehension of song texts, books and TV programs and working with computers appear to be the advantages with which the students most agree. That some things might sound better in English or that it is possible that some things cannot be expressed adequately in the national language are not really regarded as advantages.

Table 4.12

Opinions of the students on advantages of knowing English with the mean (m), the standard deviation (s.d.) and the number of students on which the means are based (N)

Advantages of knowing English	Research groups													Total sample	
	Nn (N=767)		Nb (N=321)		Bd (N=205)		Bf (N=117)		G (N=624)		F (N=142)		(N=2176)	
	m	s.d.	m	s.d.	m	s.d.	m	s.d.	m	s.d.	m	s.d.	m	s.d.
Communication abroad	3.8	.4	3.8	.4	3.9	.4	3.9	.4	3.8	.4	3.8	.5	3.8	.4
Comprehension of song texts	3.4	.7	3.4	.6	3.6	.5	3.2	.6	3.3	.8	3.1	.7	3.4	.7
Facilitation of computer work	3.4	.8	3.4	.7	3.5	.7	3.1	.8	3.1	.9	2.8	.9	3.2	.9
Facilitation of conversation	3.0	.9	3.2	.8	2.9	.8	3.1	.8	2.2	1.0	2.6	1.0	2.8	1.0
Things sound better in English	2.5	1.0	2.7	1.0	2.9	.9	2.6	.8	2.4	1.0	2.0	.8	2.5	1.0
No expression in national language	2.0	.9	2.2	1.0	2.4	.9	2.1	.9	2.5	.9	1.6	.8	2.2	1.0
Necessary for further education	3.0	.9	2.9	.9	2.9	.9	3.0	.9	3.6	.6	3.3	.8	3.2	.9
Better chance to get a good job	2.8	.9	3.2	.8	3.4	.7	3.5	.7	3.6	.7	3.1	.9	3.2	.9
Possibility to read books in English*	3.6	.6	3.8	.5	-	-	3.4	.6	2.8	1.0	3.3	.8	3.3	.9
Understand English TV programs without subtitles*	3.4	.7	3.7	.5	-	-	3.1	.7	3.1	.9	3.1	.9	3.3	.8

*The last two questions were only present in the second version of the questionnaire; therefore data are not available for the Flemish group, and only available for a part of the students in the two Dutch groups. For these questions N=553 for the Nn group, 266 for the Nb group and 1702 for the total sample.

4.3.7   English language proficiency

In order to learn more about language proficiency among the teenagers in our study, three sets of data were gathered: (1) global self-assessment of speaking, listening, writing and reading skills; (2) self-assessment using can-do scales; and (3) an English vocabulary test. The results of a fourth measure, namely the grade for English from the previous school year, are not presented in the table for a number of reasons. One is that the grading scales differ across the four countries: In the Netherlands and Wallonia the scale is 1-10; in Flanders it is 1-100; in Germany it is 1-6; and in France, 1-20. We tried to translate the different systems into one scale by means of marking conversion tables used in student exchange programs (e.g., Erasmus) of the European Community, but then it still remains rather difficult to decide if differences in scores found between groups are real or due to the conversion process. Another difficulty is that the precise meaning of a grade in terms of proficiency in English depends on the school level: a student with a grade of 5 (good) in class 4 will be (or one would assume to be) more proficient in English than a student with the same grade in class 3. In other words, grades as an index for relative proficiency (good, bad) in English are valid only in relation to the forms and school types pupils are in.

4.3.7.1 Global self-assessments

On this measure, a 4-point scale ranging from *bad* (1) to *good* (4) was used for five of the six groups. For the Bf group, responses were given on a 7-point scale with the range *unsatisfactory* the lowest rating (1) and *excellent* the highest (4). In order to compute the means of the four skill areas for all six groups, the 7-point scale was adapted to a 4-point scale. In general, the results show self-estimations of listening and reading proficiency to be higher than the outcome for speaking and writing (see Table 4.13). The Nb group and Bf group have the highest mean scores overall.

Table 4.13
Self assessment for speaking, listening, writing and reading with the mean (m), the standard deviation (s.d.) and the number of students who answered the question (N)

Research groups	Speaking			Listening			Writing			Reading		
	m	s.d.	N	m	s.d.	N	m	s.d.	N	m	s.d.	N
Nn	3.1	.6	785	3.3	.7	781	2.9	.7	781	3.2	.7	780
Nb	3.3	.6	328	3.7	.5	328	3.3	.6	328	3.6	.5	328
Bd	2.9	.7	206	3.2	.7	204	2.8	.7	203	3.1	.7	203
Bf	3.3	.7	118	3.1	1.0	118	3.5	.7	118	3.7	.7	118
G	2.9	.8	636	3.2	.7	631	2.9	.8	629	3.2	.8	631
F	2.3	.8	144	2.4	.8	145	2.4	.8	146	2.6	.8	144
Total sample	3.0	.7	2217	3.2	.7	2207	3.0	.8	2205	3.2	.7	2204

4.3.7.2 "Can do" assessment

The "can do" assessment consisted of a list of short descriptions for 34 communicative tasks that were evaluated according to the extent that the pupils could perform each particular task. In the administration, the statements were arranged randomly; the response scale ranged from 4 (*easily*) to 1 (*probably impossible*). For analysis, the statements were grouped by the traditional four skill areas of speaking, listening, reading/writing and, within skill areas, the findings were sorted in ascending order of difficulty experienced by the total sample (See Appendix D for details).

The ordering by difficulty is globally the same within all groups. For speaking, the order from *easy* to *very difficult* is: (1) Simple everyday situations; (2) Everyday conversations; and, (3) Complex (more formal) conversation; for listening, the order is: (1) Easy listening (simple situations/adjusted speech); (2) Everyday listening (speech not adjusted, but content related to areas of interest to students in that age); and, (3) More complex/formal situations.

For the Nb group the scores are, again, the highest overall (with none of the mean scores below 3, *rather difficult*, and for the F group overall the lowest (this is the only group with mean scores that are below 2, *very difficult*, for many statements).

4.3.7.3 Vocabulary test

The third measure of English proficiency from which we obtained results on language proficiency was the vocabulary test. This test of passive word knowledge in English was used with all groups except the French group. As Table 4.14 shows, the Nb group and the Bf group appear to have the highest mean score. Overall, differences in mean score seem to correspond to the differences in school types attended by the pupils. However, the higher education level of the Bf group is not reflected in their results on this test.

Table 4.14
Scores on the EFL Vocabulary Test with the mean,
the standard deviation (s.d.) and the number of
students who completed the test.

		Score on the EFL Vocabulary Test		
		mean	s.d.	N
Research groups	Nn	62.2	17.7	763
	Nb	85.6	9.3	225
	Bd	76.6	10.4	208
	Bf	56.7	17.3	118
	G	52.9	14.4	624
	F	-	-	-
Total sample		63.1	18.5	1938

Table 4.15 displays data on the relative contribution of school media and other sources for acquiring English as assessed by the pupils themselves.

Table 4.15
Acquisition of the English language: portions in percent attributed by the students to
school media and other sources, with the mean, the standard deviation (s.d.) and the
number of students from whom data are available (N)

			Acquisition of English					
			% through school		% through media		% other ways	
		N	mean	s.d.	mean	s.d.	mean	s.d.
Research groups	Nn	759	58.2	20.7	29.9	18.4	11.9	14.7
	Nb	328	58.8	22.1	23.2	16.1	18.0	19.3
	Bd	183	59.6	21.1	36.7	20.7	3.8	8.8
	Bf	117	77.5	16.4	12.8	10.8	9.7	12.0
	G	602	72.7	19.4	16.4	14.8	10.9	14.3
	F	143	82.6	18.2	7.6	10.4	9.8	14.5
Total. sample		2132	65.2	21.9	23.2	18.4	11.6	15.2

In all groups the school is seen as the most important source; however, its portion varies from about 60% in Dutch-speaking groups to about 80% in French-speaking groups. In all groups, except the French, school is followed by the media. In the three Dutch-speaking groups, in particular, the proportion is rather substantial (about a quarter for students in bilingual schools to a third for Belgian speakers of Dutch). The option *other ways* was most important for Dutch students in bilingual schools, and least important for Belgian speakers of Dutch (18% and 3.8%, respectively), and around 10% for the other four groups.

Up to this point, the analyses in this chapter have focussed on the main findings from the questionnaire and the proficiency tests. These different sets of data in their present form are in themselves interesting, but due to the large number and variety of questions, it is difficult to get a good overall picture. Therefore, it is useful to draw profiles of different groups on relevant variables (See Appendix E for presentation of all the main variables.)

Both the Nb and the Bd group tend to have parents with a higher level of education, parents and siblings with higher levels of proficiency, more contact with English through media and contacts, and they show higher scores on the proficiency tests. For the German and French groups, the scores are more varied, so they have less contact with English and they show lower proficiency scores. To what extent these characteristics can be related to language proficiency scores will be considered in the next chapter.

Chapter 5

DETERMINANTS OF CONTACT, PROFICIENCY, AND ATTITUDES

Kees de Bot and Riet Evers

5.1   INTRODUCTION

This chapter is an analysis of how the variables described in the previous chapter are causally related. As such it includes a rather technical, but unavoidably so, account of the various statistical procedures and decisions made in the process of running the data and in interpreting the results, which may make part of the chapter less accessible to readers without a background in statistics (See Chapter 7 for a non-technical discussion of the findings).

Given the very large number of variables in our study, we had to restrict the analysis to the main variables. We concentrate on a limited number of variables, in particular, contact with the English language (Contact), language (Proficiency), attitudes towards the English language (Attitudes), and the role of a number of variables in the family setting (Family Background).

The following considerations were made in excluding other variables: In the first global analyses, school and class variables appeared to be too heterogeneous to be included. Also for some of the variables, the number of pupils in various countries was so low that an analysis aimed at generalization would be unwarranted. With respect to the class variables, the range was larger in the Dutch sample and the German sample than in the Belgian and French. Therefore, for some school types no conclusions can be drawn for the latter groups.

Our main question - what influences what? - has no simple answer because the type of study we have carried out, which is basically a one-shot study without repeated measurements over time, does not permit us to explain changes diachronically. Although we have data from various class and age groups, the dataset is incomplete for all groups.   Therefore, this study cannot be presented as being cross-sectional.

The three questions addressed in the analysis were:

1. What are the scores of the six groups for the four main variables - Contact, Proficiency, Attitudes and Family Background - and to what extent are there differences between the groups?

2. What is the causal relation between these four main variables?

3. Can one single explanatory model be used for all six groups involved and, if not, on what variables do the groups differ?

In order to answer each of these questions, separate analyses were carried out: for question 1, analyses of variance with post-hoc testing of contrasts; for question 2, a standard LISREL analysis; and for question 3, a multi-sample LISREL analysis. For the post hoc analysis only contrasts that differed at the $p < .05$ level are noted.

The four main variables were constructed on the basis of a large number of indicators from the available data. Figure 5.1 presents the main variables and their associated indicators.

Figure5.1
Main variables and indicators
Contact
        Contact through personal backgrounds (parents, siblings, peer group);
        Contact through media I: TV, film, music;
        Contact through media II: Radio/spoken, journals, newspapers (reduced by means
        of a factor-analysis (principle component analysis with oblimin rotation) and taking
        the means for the variables with high loadings (>.40), scale 1-4
        Contact through holidays, reduced to 7 categories, scale 0-6
Proficiency
        Self assessment (Mean scores can-do scales), scale 1-4
        Meara EFL Vocabulary test, scale .00 - .99
Attitudes
        Likeability of English, scale 1-4
        Importance of English, scale 1-4
        Mean of main advantages of knowing English, scale 1-4
Family background
        Level of education, parents (3 categories: low, medium, high, highest level of both
        parents), scale 1-3
        English language proficiency, parents (mean for both parents), scale 1-7
        English language proficiency, siblings (mean for siblings older than 5), scale 1-7

In the analyses presented in this chapter, not all pupils have been included for a variety of reasons. First, since there were no first graders in any of the other groups, Nn first graders were excluded; second, because all of the analyses were done list-wise and part of the data were missing - in particular for level of education of parents and vocabulary test scores - fairly large numbers of pupils had to be excluded, amounting to 60% of the Nb pupils and 24% of the G pupils.

Based upon post-hoc analyses between the pupils that were included and those that were excluded, we found no real differences between these two groups. Therefore, we believed it could reasonably be assumed that the exclusion of part of the pupils did not lead to any specific bias in the outcomes.

5.2   GROUP SCORES ON VARIABLES AND EXTENT OF DIFFERENCES (QUESTION A)

What are the scores of the six groups of pupils for the indicator variables of the four main variables of Contact, Proficiency, Attitudes and Family Background?

To answer this question, mean scores for indicators per group were calculated and differences between groups analyzed using analyses of variance and post-hoc tests (Tamhane). The results are presented in Tables 5.1 and 5.2 (main variables and their associated indicators).

Note that as in previous chapters the following labels have been used:
Nn   Dutch students following normal education
Nb   Dutch students following bilingual (Dutch/English) education
Bd   Belgian Dutch-speaking students
Bf   Belgian French-speaking students
G   German students
F   French students

Table 5.1

Results analyses of variance

	F	Df	p	Eta^2	Significant differences between groups (p=.05, Tamhane)
Family variables					
Education level of parents	41.65	5, 1564	.000	.118	G, F ≤ F, Nn < Bd, Nb, Bf
English proficiency of parents	98.39	5, 1564	.000	.239	
English proficiency of siblings	19.24	5, 1564	.000	.058	F < Bf, G < Nn, Bd, Nb Bf, F, G < Nn, Nb, Bd
Contact with English					
Through family/friends	17.45	5, 1564	.000	.053	F < G, Bd, Bf ≤ Bd, Bf, Nn < Nb
Through media music/film	115.86	5, 1564	.000	.270	F < Bf, G < Nn, Bd ≤ Bd, Nb
Through media info	39.24	5, 1564	.000	.111	Bf, F, Bd ≤ F, Bd, Nn < Nb < G
Through use in vacations	22.46	5, 1564	.000	.067	F < Bd, Bf < Nn, G < Nb
Proficiency in English					
Self-assessment	112.47	5, 1564	.000	.264	F < Bf < Bd, G, Nn < Nb
Vocabulary test	192.94	4, 1436	.000	.350	G, Bf < Nn < Bd < Nb*
Attitudes towards English					
Estimation	18.67	5, 1564	.000	.056	F < G, Nn, < Bd, Nb, Bf
Importance	26.85	5, 1564	.000	.079	F < Nn < Bf, G, Nb, Bd
Advantages	16.79	5, 1564	.000	.051	F < Nn, Bf, G, Nb ≤ Nb, Bd

* Scores on the vocabulary test are missing for the French group

< = groups before this sign have a score that is significantly lower than the one for the group after the sign, so F < G means that the F group has a score that is significantly lower than G group score

≤ = A group that appears both before and after the sign does not differ significantly from the other groups before or after the sign. Groups appearing before the sign have scores that are significantly lower. So G, F ≤ F; Nn means that G and F do not differ significantly, nor dc F and Nn, but G and Nn do differ.

Table 5.2
Results for main variables in groups

	Nn		Nb		Bd		Bf		G		F	
	mean	sd	mean	sd	mean	sd	mean	sd	mean	sd	mean	sd
Family variables												
education level of parents	2.01	.71	2.48	.64	2.34	.80	2.59	.68	1.75	.86	1.83	.71
English proficiency of parents	5.23	1.08	5.51	1.02	5.26	.95	3.85	1.60	4.27	1.65	2.91	1.40
English proficiency of siblings	4.59	1.66	4.67	1.86	4.81	1.49	3.41	1.93	3.91	1.98	3.76	1.76
Contact with English												
through family/friends	1.78	.55	2.01	.71	1.69	.51	1.73	.52	1.65	.50	1.45	.42
through media: music/film	3.39	.55	3.57	.48	3.43	.56	2.85	.57	2.93	.52	2.43	.53
through media: info	1.72	.51	1.88	.50	1.62	.54	1.47	.44	2.05	.66	1.55	.51
through use in vacations	1.57	1.63	2.43	1.71	1.07	1.04	1.14	1.27	1.67	1.65	.68	1.03
Proficiency in English												
Self-assessment mean score	3.08	.45	3.59	.30	3.04	.44	2.79	.39	3.07	.47	2.31	.55
vocabulary test	.67	.15	.85	.10	.77	.10	.56	.17	.54	.14	--	--
Attitude												
Estimation of English	3.19	.66	3.47	.58	3.38	.57	3.53	.57	3.12	.86	2.81	.85
Importance of English	3.42	.64	3.68	.50	3.77	.46	3.64	.52	3.66	.59	3.14	.75
Advantages	3.01	.47	3.12	.42	3.19	.40	3.05	.40	3.06	.45	2.75	.41

5.3   CONTACT WITH ENGLISH

Overall, we find that the possibilities for out-of-school contact with the English language are most limited for the F group, while the Nb group has the most opportunity for contact. For all groups, audio-visual media are the most important source of contact. For the total group the mean score for this variable is slightly higher than 3, which indicates frequent contact via AV media.

5.3.1   Personal networks

The Nb group showed the highest score, followed by the Nn, Bf, and Bd groups. Of these three groups only the Nn group had a higher score than the G group, which in turn had a higher score than the F group. Only for the Nb group the mean frequency was *sometimes*; for the other groups the mean was lower.

5.3.2   Media I

Music, film, TV: For the Dutch-speaking groups the mean frequency was between *often* and *very often*, the Nb group showed a higher score than the Nn group. For the other groups the score ranged from *sometimes* to *often*, with higher scores for the G group than the F group.

5.3.3   Media II

Radio, newspapers, journals: In contrast to the other contact variables, the G group had the highest scores on this indicator. Scores were generally low; only the G group was slightly above *sometimes*. The Dutch-speaking groups had higher scores than the F group. Within the Dutch-speaking groups the Nb group typically had the highest scores.

5.3.4   Vacations

The F groups showed significantly lower scores than both B groups, which in turn had lower scores than the Nn and G groups. Again, the Nb had the highest score with a mean between 2 (3 to 4 times) and 3 (5 to 7 times). In contrast, the scores for the F groups were between 0 (never) and 1 (1 to 2 times).

5.4   PROFICIENCY IN ENGLISH

5.4.1   "Can do" Scales

The F group appeared to have the most difficulties in dealing with the situations presented to them on the "can do" scale. For this group the means ranged from *difficult* to *very difficult*. Next is the Bf group who still found dealing with the situations *rather difficult*. The G, Bd and Nn groups had scores around *rather difficult*, while the Nb group showed means between *rather difficult* and *easy*.

5.4.2   Vocabulary test

The scores on this test differ from those on the self-evaluations. Here, the G and Bf groups have the lowest scores, followed by the Nn group and then the Bd group.   In order to compare the two variables, the scores were recalculated on a scale from 0-100. Table 5.3 presents the means on this scale and the correlation between the two indicators.

Table 5.3
Proficiency scores in percentages

	Nn		Nb		Bd		Bf		G		F	
	mean	sd	mean	sd	mean	sd	mean	sd	mean	sd	mean	sd
Self-assessment	69.2	14.9	86.4	9.9	68.1	14.8	59.7	13.0	69.1	15.8	43.7	18.3
Vocabulary test	66.8	14.9	85.4	10.1	76.6	10.2	56.1	17.1	53.7	14.2	--	--
Correlation	.35**		.43**		.32**		.31**		.32**		--	

The correlation coefficients show a significant but not very high correlation between self assessment and the vocabulary test. This is the pattern that is normally found in such comparisons and it suggests some overlap between the underlying constructs measured, as well as a specific contribution from each of the indicators. Correlations are highest and the differences between the self-evaluations and vocabulary test are lowest for the Nb group. Only the mean score for the self-evaluations of the Bd group is lower than the mean scores on the vocabulary test. All other groups show the opposite pattern, and the difference is largest for the G group.

5.5   ATTITUDES TOWARD ENGLISH

5.5.1   Likeability of English

The F group appears to like English the least, and this suggests a negative attitude toward English. This group is the only one with a score below *rather like it* while all other groups appear to be more positively inclined. For the high-scoring groups – Bd, Nb and Bf – the scores range from *rather like it* to *like it very much*. The contrast between the F and Bf group is salient here: apparently it is not the mother tongue that plays a major role in the attitudes, and it may be that social attitudes play a role as suggested by differences between Belgium's and France's treatment of loanwords (see Chapter 2).

5.5.2   Importance of English

All groups think it is important to have a good command of English. The F group shows the lowest score but this is still above *rather important*. Among the four remaining groups, the Nn group has the next lowest score.

5.5.3   Advantages of knowing English

All groups *rather agree* with the advantages given on the survey. The F groups had the lowest scores, while the Nb had the highest scores, followed by the Bd group.

5.6   FAMILY BACKGROUND

5.6.1   Educational level of parents

For the two Belgian groups and the Nb group the mean level of education of the parents appears to be higher than for the other groups. The F and G groups show the lowest scores. The differences between the groups are probably related to the school types of the different countries included in the survey: The F group comprised vocational training only while the B and Nb groups were all preparing for university studies.

5.6.2   English proficiency of parents

The pupils in the Dutch speaking groups estimate the level of English proficiency of their parents to be significantly higher than the other groups. The mean scores for both parents are between *rather good* and *good*. For the

F group the score is even below *bad*; the Bf and G groups show mean levels of proficiency around *rather bad*.

5.6.3 English proficiency of siblings

The estimated level of proficiency for siblings is significantly higher for the Dutch speaking groups, as it was for their parents. For these groups the mean level is between *rather bad* and *rather good*. For the Bf, F and G groups they were between *bad* and *rather bad*.

The pattern of this analysis, which is based on a reduced sample, is basically the same as that presented for the total group in Chapter 4.

5.7 MAIN VARIABLES AND CAUSAL RELATION (QUESTION B)

In this project there were many variables which made it difficult at times to see the forest for the trees. Relations between all variables could be put in a large correlation matrix that shows the strength of the relations between the variables, but that would hardly make the outcomes more transparent. There are several statistical techniques en programs that can help us to reduce the number variables by bringing them together, but there is little point in doing this purely on the basis of the statistics, because some relations or combinations of variables may be statistically relevant, but conceptually nonsensical. Therefore, it is better to start with a conceptual organization of different parts of the data on theoretical (or common sense) grounds. Of course, a project like the one presented here didn't start as a set of correlating variables, but out of an interest in different factors that may play a role on language proficiency in the groups studied. There was a conceptual structure to start with and in the analysis that structure needs to be taken into account. As indicated earlier there were 4 main sets of variables: Contact with English; Socio-economic and educational status of family; Attitudes towards English; and English proficiency

For each of these sets there were questions in the questionnaire or tests that have been administered. So , for instance the score for English proficiency was based on data from the Self-assessment instrument and the Vocabulary test, while attitudes towards English was constructed on the basis of data on Attractiveness of English, Importance of English and Advantages of knowing English.

The first step in the analysis now is to indicate how the four sets of variables are related. This means that we have to have an idea of the *direction* of relations between sets: what is likely to cause what? In our project this is not an easy question: contact with English will probably have an impact on attitudes towards English, but it is also possible that a positive attitude towards English leads to more contacts with English. Similarly, Socio-economic and educational status of the family is likely to have an impact on proficiency in English, but it may also be, though less likely, that higher English proficiency leads to higher socio-economic status, e.g. because a good command of English provides access to better paid jobs. There are two ways to go: one is to accept that sets of variables are correlated but not predicting the direction of the effect, the other is to assume directions of effect and test them statistically. There are good arguments for both solutions, and the reality probably is that all these sets of variables interact and influence each other over time. Here we have chosen for a solution in which we take one set of variables as the dependent variable and the other sets as independent variables. In our analysis we tested two models: model 1 in which attitudes towards English is the dependent variable and model 2 in which English proficiency is the dependent variable. The two options are visualized in Figure 5.2. In order to test the assumed relations, we carried out LISREL analyses (Jöreskog & Sörbom, 1981, version 8.13).

The aim of such models is to find a hypothetical structure of relations, that is, theoretically plausible patterns of coherence between variables which show an optimal "fit" with empirically-established statistical relations between variables. "Fit" here means the configuration of variables that best explains the results. With the LISREL program such patterns can be established and tested. In a first model the variables and all theoretically postulated relations between variables are presented in a diagram with arrows. On the basis of the outcomes of the analysis, the model is specified further and variables and relations that were included in the first model can be eliminated in subsequent models; new variables and relations can be added also. The adequacy of such adaptations can be tested with the program using different measures of fit.

The most important step that precedes the analysis proper is the choice of a model. We intended to test three models that seemed plausible to us on theoretical grounds: Model 1, in which Proficiency is the final dependent variable; Model 2, in which Attitudes are the final dependent variable; and, Model 3, a mixed model in which a reciprocal relation between Attitudes and Proficiency is included. A fourth possible model would be to take "contact" as the dependent variable, but given the rather fixed settings of the students in our study this was not a relevant model to explore.

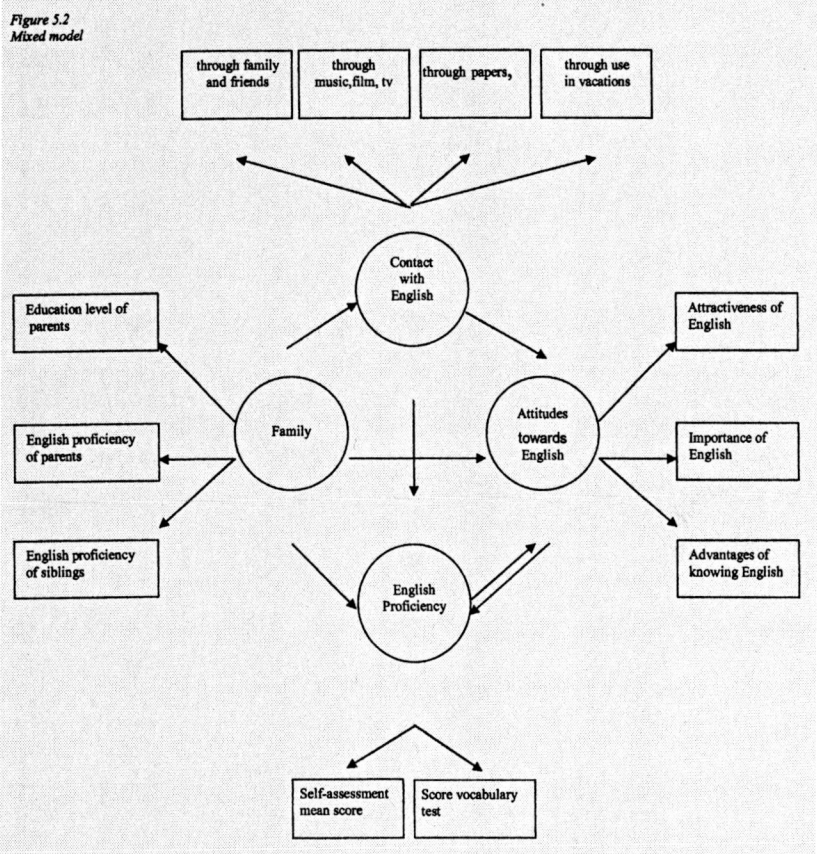

Figure 5.2
Mixed model

Model 1

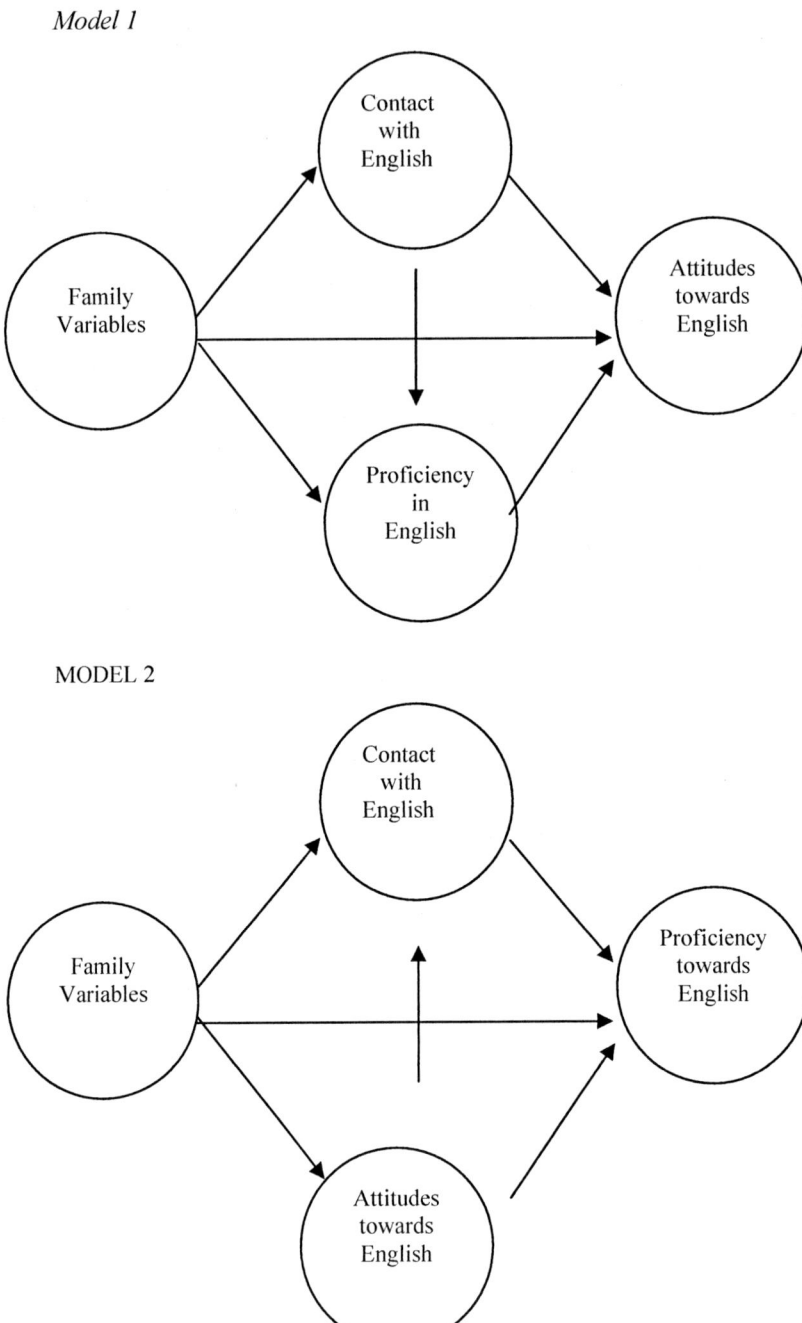

MODEL 2

Given the differences between groups, the explanatory variable group was included in the model with five dummy variables (variables that have to be included in order to perform the analysis) and the Nn group as a reference category. So it was tested whether and how all the other groups differed from the reference group. It should be noted that this was a highly arbitrary choice. We could also have taken the optimal group Nb as a reference for the comparison between groups. Since none of the pupils in the F group had been administered the vocabulary test, and we still wanted to include them in the overall analysis, we took the mean scores of the other pupils (the mean of the means of the other groups) as the score for this group.

The result of the analysis of the two remaining models showed that Model 2, with attitudes as the dependent variable, was to be preferred because the effects were more pronounced than in Model 3, which takes proficiency as the dependent variable. The results of the analysis of Model 1 are presented in Table 5.4. For the purpose of clarity, only the standardized estimates have been included in the table and the effects of the group variable have been excluded. The complete unstandardized data can be found in Appendix G.

In the tables, the dash (-) indicates an effect that is postulated in the model, but non-significant and therefore fixed at 0. An empty cell indicates that for these variables no effect was postulated in the model, therefore they have also been fixed at 0 at the beginning of the analysis. The usual measures of goodness of fit are satisfactory for this model (X^2 [df=22] = 32.55, p=.067, adjusted goodness of fit index [AGFI] =.99 [maximum = 1, criterion for fit: values > .95], standardized root mean square residual [RMR] = .007).

In Table 5.4 both the direct and the total effects are presented. Direct effects refer to the effect of one variable on another variable without an intervening variable, e.g. the relation between Self-assessment and English proficiency of parents. Total effects refer to the combination of direct and indirect effects, e.g. the relation between Self-Assessment and English proficiency, directly but also through other variables, such as Attitudes towards English. The total effect is larger (.16) than the direct effect (.07) which shows that the two variables are both directly and indirectly related.

Table 5.4
Family variables, contact, and proficiency.
Direct and total effects: standardized estimates for total sample (N=1570)

	FAMILY VARIABLES			CONTACT				PROFICIENCY		R²
	EduPar	EngPar	EngSib	Fa/fr	Media1	Media2	Vac	SA	Voc	
Direct effects										
CONTACT										
Family/friends	--	.20***	.22***							
Media 1	--	.09***	.13***							
Media:2	--	.12***	.11***							
Vacations	.08**	.23***	.07**							
PROFICIENCY										
Self-assessment	.06*	.07**	.05*	.17***	.16***	.09***	.11***			
Vocabulary test	.09***	--	--	.05*	.10***	--	.08***			
ATTITUDES										
Estimation	--	--	--	.09***	.09***	--	--	.47***	.07**	
Importance	--	--	--	.10***	.11***	--	--	.28***	--	
Advantages	--	--	--	.09***	.17***	.07**	--	.23***	--	
Total effects										
CONTACT										
Family/friends	--	.20***	.22***							.14
Media:music/film	--	.09***	.13***							.30
Media: info	--	.12***	.11***							.13
Vacations	.08**	.23***	.07**							.13
PROFICIENCY										
Self-assessment	.07**	.16***	.12***	.17***	.16***	.09***	.11***			.40
Vocabulary test	.10***	.04***	.03***	.05*	.10***	--	.08***			.38
ATTITUDES										
Estimation	.04***	.10***	.09***	.18***	.17***	.04***	.06***	.47***	.07**	.30
Importance	.02**	.07***	.07***	.14***	.15***	.02***	.03***	.28***	--	.18
Advantages	.02**	.08***	.08***	.13***	.20***	.09***	.03***	.23***	--	.18

The model can be described by looking at the various effects as follows:

Family Background - Contact: It appears that the impact of level of parents' and siblings' proficiency is far more important than the parents' level of education. This latter variable appears to have a major impact on use of English during vacations. Siblings' level of English appears to have somewhat more influence on contact with English through music and films than parents' English proficiency. In all cases, more frequent use of English is associated with higher level of proficiency of parents.

Family Background - Proficiency: Proficiency of both parents and siblings appears to affect pupils' self-evaluations on the "can do" scales. In contrast, for the vocabulary test the level of parents' education plays a role as well, but both effects are relatively small.

Family Background - Attitudes: None of the three Family Background variables appear to influence attitudes, but there is a weak indirect relation through Contact and Proficiency variables.

Contact - Proficiency: Contact through personal network, media I and vacations has a direct effect on both self-evaluations and vocabulary scores. Media II has an effect on self-evaluations only. Also, for the other three indicators, the effect is much stronger for self-evaluations than for the vocabulary scores. Contacts through personal network and through music and TV appear to be most influential.

Contact - Attitudes: The use of English during vacations appears to have no effect on attitudes. There is a clear effect of contact through personal network and in particular through music/TV on likeability and importance of knowing English. Contact through Media II only affects the extent to which advantages of knowing English are mentioned.

Proficiency - Attitudes: Overall the effect of self-evaluations on attitudes is much stronger than the effect of vocabulary knowledge. Language proficiency as measured by the vocabulary test has an effect only on likeability, but here the effect of self-evaluations is also stronger.

5.8   AN EXPLANATORY MODEL FOR ALL GROUPS (QUESTION C)

To what extent can we use one single explanatory model for all groups involved?

In order to answer this question, LISREL analyses with a multi-sample approach were conducted. With this approach the validity of a model can be tested for different groups in an integral way. Question C was split into two sub-questions:

Sub-question 1: Is the pattern of causal relations found for the total sample the same as the one found for each of the six groups?

Sub-question 2: If there are differences, on what variables do we see them?

As in the prior analysis, the covariances were used as a measure of coherence. For the F group the mean score on the missing vocabulary test was fixed at 0.

Same pattern (Subquestion 1): The statistics for goodness of fit show that the same patterns of causal relations were found for all groups (X^2 [df=132] = 184.44, p=.002, GFI=.98, standardized RMR=.03, ratio X^2/DF= 1.40, ratio X^2/D=1.48).

Identical effects: (subquestion 2) When the model is tested not just for identity of pattern but also for identity of effects, it shows a satisfactory overall fit (X^2 [df=287] = 465.48, p=.001, GFI=.97, standardized RMR=.06, ratio X^2/df=1.62). However, additional measures of fit focusing on specific effects suggest that the explanatory model with respect to individual effects is exactly the same for all groups. Therefore, we searched for models that not only deviate as little as possible from the general model, but do that justice as well to the differences found. The results from this multi-sample model are presented in Table 5.5. In this table the unstandardized estimates of the direct effects have been included. (The estimates of the total effects can be found in Appendix G.)

Table 5.5
Multisample Analysis: unstandardized estimates of total effects

	Family Variables			Contact				Proficiency	
	EduPar	EngPar	EngSib	Fa/fr	Media 1	Media 2	Vac	SA	Voc
Contact									
Family/friends	--	.07***	.07***						
Media 1	--	.04***	.04***						
Media 2	--	.04***	.03***						
Vacations	.12*	.22***	.06**						
Proficiency									
Self-assessment	.04**	.05***	.04*** .01 (2,4)	.14***	.13***	.09***	.03***		
Vocabulary test	.02*** -- (6)	.00*** .00** (2,3) -- (6)	.00*** .00 (3) -- (6)	.02* -.02* (3) -- (6)	.03*** -- (6)	--	.01*** -- (6)		
Attitudes									
Estimation	.04*** .02 (2) .02***(4) .03** (6)	.05*** .04***(2) .03***(4)	.04*** .02***(2,4)	.23*** .22***(2,3) .17***(4)	.23*** .19**(2) .17***(4) .21***(6)	.06*** .02***(4)	.03*** .02***(2) .01***(4) .02***(6)	.66*** .21***(4)	.44*** -.69***(2)
Importance	.01** .00 (3) .03***(5)	.03** .01 (3) .06***(6)	.02** (1,4) .01 (2,3) .03** (5) .06***(6)	.13 .08 (3) .14 (5) .61***(6)	.16*** .11***(3) .18**(5)	.03*** .00 (3)	.01*** .00 (3) .02**(5)	.33*** -.03 (3)	.62***(5)
Advantages	.01** .02** (2)	.02*** .03***(1) .04***(2)	.02*** .01***(3,4)	.09*** .11***(1) .15***(2)	.15*** .17***(1) .20***(2)	.07*** .08***(1) .10***(2)	.00*** .01***(1) .02***(2)	.13*** .30***(1) .55***(2)	--

1=Nn, 2=Nb, 3=Bd, 4=Bf, 5=G, 6=F
*=p<.05, **=p<.01, ***=p<.001

This model shows an acceptable fit (X^2 [df=277] = 357.90, p=.001, GFI=.98, standardized RMR=.047, ratio X^2/df=1.29). A total of 10 adaptations were needed. In almost all cases the discrepancies resulted from effects that were stronger (3x) or that were either not at all or less significant (6x) in one of the groups as compared to the groups taken together.

Nn group: 1 adaptation. The effect of the self-assessment scores on advantages of English appeared to be stronger for this group than for the B, F and G groups.

Nb group: 3 adaptations. For this group, no effect was found for the siblings' level of English on the self-assessment scores and for the vocabulary scores on the likeability of English. In both cases the effect was positive for the other groups, while for the Nb group these relations seemed to be rather negative. This is particularly so in the relation between vocabulary scores and likeability, which is probably not significant within group Nb because of a rather high standard of error. On the other hand, the effect of the self-assessment scores on advantages of English appeared to be much stronger for this group than for all other groups.

Bd group: 2 adaptations. No effect was found for contact through family/friends on the vocabulary scores and for the self-assessment scores on the importance of English.

Bf group: 2 adaptations. As with the Nb group, no effect was found for the English proficiency of siblings on the self-assessment score. For the self-assessment scores no effect was found on the likeability of English.

G group: 1 adaptation: For this group an effect which was not present in the total sample was included (effect of the vocabulary scores on importance of English).

F group: 1 adaptation. For this group, the effect of contact with English through family and friends on the importance of English appeared to be much stronger than for the other groups.

5.9   CONCLUSION

The structural model presented here explains relations between large sets of variables in different groups. It turned out that on the whole a model that takes attitudes as the dependent variable and Contact, Proficiency and Family Background as independent variables best explains the data. This appeared to be true for the total group and for the six subgroups, though there were some differences on specific variables for individual subgroups.

Chapter 6

English, Youth, and Media Environments

Uwe Hasebrink

6.1 INTRODUCTION

So far, the comparative research presented has concentrated on descriptive data on contacts with English, on language proficiency, and media use (see Chapter 4); and a linear model has been developed and tested which explains the variance of attitudes towards English by means of family variables, contacts with English and English proficiency (Chapter 5). This chapter will go one step beyond that, which means one step closer to the context of young people's everyday lives.

Research which aimed at analyzing media effects in terms of clear causal relationships between independent variables (e.g., the amount of television use) and dependent variables (e.g., proficiency in English) has not been very successful in the past. There is broad consensus in the literature that the model of direct media effects, according to which media characteristics – as determinants – directly lead to specific attitudinal or behavioral effects on the side of the audience, is unsuitable. It is by far too simplistic and thus inappropriate to deal with the complex interdependencies between media use and other areas of behavior (e.g., Webster, 1998). One main argument maintains that the actual media which people use are to a large extent their own selections: the users compose their personal media environment, an individual composition of media offerings. The notion of media environments emphasizes that even when the researcher's interest is in the particular role of a specific medium (e.g., television or the internet), one important concern is how this medium is embedded in the use of the whole media ensemble. Thus, to study the correlation between media use and language acquisition, the full media environment of a person needs to be examined together with other activities which in turn are understood in terms of specific media-related styles (Hawkins, Reynolds & Pingree, 1991;

Rosengren, 1994). It is necessary to analyze individual patterns of media use, as described, for example, in relation to TV by Hasebrink (1997) and Krotz & Hasebrink (1998). These patterns are based on the assumption that it is the individual who constructs sense and meaning in the organization of his or her life. Yet, an individual is not unique in his or her construction of reality. It is possible to construct various types of media users, which differ with regard to their media environments and which may be compared both within and between cultures.

Given these considerations, the relationship between media use and English proficiency in this chapter is not conceptualized in terms of a media effects model. Instead, the focus is differences between subgroups of young people who are living in different media environments. This approach allows for the analysis of different patterns of contact with the English language, which might be connected with different patterns of English proficiency as well.

The survey as conducted in the four countries involved in this study sets certain limits to a differentiated analysis of patterns of media use and of social background. Thus, the following analyses are necessarily explorative and not meant to provide definite results; rather, they are to increase the attention on and further the understanding of certain types of questions. Since there are just a few media-related variables in the data, the following paragraph briefly presents results of a recent study relevant to our study, namely, that done by Livingstone & Bovill (2001) on young people's changing media environments.

6.2   YOUNG PEOPLE'S MEDIA ENVIRONMENTS

With regard to the deep changes in global media landscapes there are different hypotheses about the consequences of young people's media use. Young people in contemporary Europe may be selective in their media use, either favoring only certain media and discarding others, or combining different media and adding new ones to their individual menu.

Livingstone and Bovill's study, based on comparative surveys conducted in 1997 and 1998 among 6-17 year-old European children and young people in twelve countries, is relevant to this hypothesis. There were research teams in Belgium (Flanders), Denmark, Finland, France, Germany, Israel, Italy, the Netherlands, Spain, Sweden, Switzerland, and the United Kingdom. In each of the countries involved (except Denmark), one step of the research was a survey among around 1,200 children and young people using the same questionnaire. Because of the sample size, separated analyses could be calculated for subgroups, for example, the 14-16 year-olds who can be compared with the sample of the current study.

The questionnaire covered the following areas, amongst others: use of a broad range of media, focusing questions on the use of computers and internet; attitudes towards new technologies; and, parents' attitudes towards new technologies. One analytical perspective was to identify different patterns of media use; the basis of analysis was the amount of time devoted to the different media. One important result of this analysis was that the relations between different media were quite similar between countries; thus, it was possible to identify similar clusters of children and young people which could be described as types of media users, each of which is characterized by a specific media environment (see Johnsson-Smaragdi, 2001; Johnsson-Smaragdi, d'Haenens, Krotz & Hasebrink, 1998).

According to Johnsson-Smaragdi's analyses of the data from the above-mentioned comparative study, television is still the dominant medium for all user types, both in terms of the number of users and the amount of viewing time. Everyone, everywhere, watches television, and television viewing makes up the bulk of individuals' media time. At the same time, new information and communication technologies are used within all user styles, though the proportions of users and the amount of time spent vary. There are tendencies towards media accumulation. In countries where access to computers and/or the internet is relatively high, such as Finland, Sweden, the Netherlands and Israel, the new media are often combined with traditional print and screen media. A concurrent trend towards increasing specialization in media use also is observable. The groups which specialize in computers, the internet, and electronic games are still small, but not insignificant. These groups may be growing quickly as new media disperse to a majority of the population. Cases of pure replacement of media are rare; instead, instances of media specialization and combination are common.

Media time is rearranged, allocating time for new media to be included in the menu. The more specialized groups are the heaviest media users. This is especially the case for groups whose specialization centers on the new media, indicating that they are expanding their total media time in order to make room for their interest in the new media, without reducing time spent with traditional media.

Tendencies point to an uneasy relationship between books and television in some countries; in other countries, the different kinds of media seem to go together quite well. Thus, slight indications of displacement from books to screen media, and also from television in favor of the internet, have been observed in some countries and in some user groups. The overall time profiles for the media use styles identified, also by Johnsson-Smaragdi, indicate that instances of simple media replacement are rare. Instead, there are instances of specialization of media use, reallocation of media time and additive media use. Single individuals may still displace certain media in favor of others, as the proportion of non-users shows, but this is not the general tendency. Rather, distinct user styles are developing as new media become available and differentially accepted by children and young people across Europe.

Johnsson-Smaragdi's (2001) analysis of young people's media use styles leads to the assumption that the different patterns of media use should be linked with different kinds of contacts with the English language and with different kinds of English proficiency. The following will work out this assumption and present some explorative analyses to illustrate its implications.

6.3 IDENTIFYING DIFFERENT MEDIA AND ENGLISH ENVIRONMENTS

6.3.1. Dimensions of contact with English

The respondents in the survey provided information on how often they have contact with English in different media and social contexts. We assumed that due to different patterns of media use, the young people in our study "created" different kinds of English environments. However, findings concerning this hypothesis were quite weak: the correlation between the amount of use of a specific medium (TV, radio, CD, PC, etc.) and the frequency of contact with English via the respective medium is low or moderate. For the total sample this correlation is low: .09 for television and .16 for radio (talk). This means that watching more television does not lead to more contact with English via television.

The only medium which constantly shows a fairly high correlation between amount of use and English contact in all research groups is the internet. In all the sub-samples this correlation is at least .32 (Nn), going up to .41 (G), .43 (Nb) or even .56 (Bf). This indicates that the use of computers is necessarily linked to contacts with English, whereas English contacts in other media are not a question of the medium, but, rather, the result of selective use of the medium.

Adopting the notion of different mediated English environments, the next step in our analysis was to identify relevant dimensions of these environments by means of factor analyses for each of the sub-samples. Table 6.1 displays the results.

Table 6.1
Dimensions of contact opportunities with the English language (factor analyses for all sub-samples and for the total sample: factor loadings)

	Total sample				Netherlands normal			Netherlands bilingual				Belgium Flanders				Belgium Wallonia					Germany				France			
N of cases	N=2.072				N=737			N=316				N=192				N=110					N=593				N=124			
Variance explained	57,6 %				48,2 %			54,7 %				56,1 %				61,6 %					48,4 %				56,4 %			
	I	II	III	IV	I	II	III	I	II	III	IV	I	II	III	IV	I	II	III	IV	V	I	II	III	IV	I	II	III	IV
Parents			.74				.72		.82				.65							.86			.70				.74	
Siblings			.78				.79		.79				.66					.72					.77				.81	
Friends			.68				.70		.57				.78					.74					.66		.48			.49
Radio music				.80	.69			.66				.74					.78					.64				.75		
CD/MC	.44			.71	.83			.80				.79					.83					.80				.83		
Music language	.61				.50			.41			-.44				-.53	.58	.49					.59				.75		
TV	.75				.63			.61				.64				.52				.44	.53				.65			
Cinema	.74				.60			.60				.67				.74					.69							
Radio words		.52		.51	.57						.71		.49						.68		.46			.83				.83
Papers		.81			.79					.72				.87		.42		-.42	.41		.82				.67			
Magazines		.75			.70					.68				.78		.72					.83				.69			
Books	.44	.43			.57					.72				.57		.55	-.42				.53							
Computers		.48			.48					.56					.77				.71		.43						.53	

The most common feature for all the sub-samples is the close link among the three non-mediated opportunities to have contact with English (parents, sibling, friends) and their formations as one single factor in almost all sub-samples – except for the French speaking. With regard to contacts with English via the media, one factor in all samples represents English contact via music (CDs, music on radio), and – when listening to music – preference for English language music.

Beyond this common finding, there is a striking difference between the Dutch-speaking samples on the one hand, and the German- and French-speaking on the other. In the Dutch-speaking countries, the music factor also includes television and cinema. Because movies are not dubbed in these countries, these entertainment media are sources of contact with English for young people.

For German- and French-speaking samples, television and cinema go together with another factor, which is strongly shaped by reading magazines, papers, and books and the computer. This combination suggests highly selective media use that leads to what can be called "intentional contact" with English, which contrasts with the everyday companionship of music media as when music playing in the background while engaged in another activity) that lead to contact with English of a more incidental nature.

In all sub-samples, most of the factor loadings as well as original correlations are positive, indicating a general "the more, the more" rule of contact with English. However, some exceptions can be explained only on an ad hoc basis. For two Dutch-speaking groups, the music language shows a substantial negative loading in addition to the normal positive loading on the music factor: in the Nb group, preference for English language lyrics is negatively correlated with contact with English via print media; in the Bf group, music language (negative loading) forms a joint factor with English contact when using the computer (positive loading). These findings could be interpreted as indicators for dissociation between preferences for globalized popular culture, on the one hand, and a more education-oriented search for information in print media and computers on the other.

Given that some sub-samples are rather small, we knew a more detailed analysis of their subparts would lead to difficulties in significance and reliability. Therefore, we limited the next step in the analysis to just the largest, that is, the Nn group and the G group, and provided factor solutions which were quite clear and easy to interpret. For each of the sub-samples we got three factors (Table 6.2): (1) The "family factor" showing almost identical factor loadings for the two samples; (2) the "music factor" including CDs, music on radio, and English song lyrics; and, (3) the "print factor". The only salient difference between the samples are the factoring together of TV and cinema with print media for the German sample, and the linking of watching subtitled English-language television programs to the music factor for the Dutch sample.

6.3.2 Sub-groups with different English environments

On the basis of the factor values described above, four clusters were identified by means of explorative cluster analysis for each of the two sub-samples from the Netherlands and Germany. (Analysis of Variance, main effect between groups, d.f. = 3, F-values at least 23,5; p<.001. We did not calculate contrasts between single groups since our focus was the pattern of each group). The underlying logic of this procedure is to build groups of respondents who are very similar within the groups, yet show clear differences between the groups. We decided on a 4-cluster solution because it seemed to be both simple and satisfactorily differentiated.

Table 6.2 shows the results. The first information shows the size of the clusters (Cl.). The next section lists the different opportunities for contacts with English. As these variables built the statistical basis for the clusters, necessarily significant differences obtain between the clusters with regard to these variables.

In the presence of English

Table 6.2
Contacts with English and other characteristics of sub-groups with different media environments

	Total	Netherlands				Total	Germany			
		Cl. N1	Cl. N2	Cl. N3	Cl. N4		Cl. G1	Cl. G2	Cl. G3	Cl. G4
No. of cases	737	172	251	165	149	593	127	141	217	108
In % of total	100	23,3	34,1	22,4	20,2	100	21,4	23,8	36,6	18,2
Contacts with English:										
Parents	1,8	**2,3**	*1,3*	2,0	1,6	1,5	**2,1**	1,4	*1,2*	1,4
Siblings	1,7	**2,3**	*1,3*	1,8	1,4	1,6	**2,4**	1,5	*1,2*	1,5
Friends	1,9	**2,3**	*1,5*	2,2	1,7	1,9	**2,6**	1,9	1,7	*1,6*
Radio music	3,4	3,5	3,6	**3,6**	*2,5*	3,5	**3,8**	3,6	3,7	*2,7*
CD/MC	3,5	3,7	**3,8**	**3,8**	*2,6*	3,6	3,7	**3,8**	**3,8**	*2,6*
Music language*	5,9	**6,1**	**6,1**	5,9	5,3	5,4	5,5	5,6	**5,7**	4,4
TV	3,4	3,5	3,6	3,7	2,8	2,6	2,8	3,1	2,3	2,0
Cinema	3,1	3,0	3,2	3,6	2,3	2,0	2,2	2,7	1,6	1,6
Radio words	1,9	1,7	1,7	**2,5**	1,7	2,4	2,7	**3,0**	2,2	1,8
Papers	1,4	*1,1*	*1,1*	**2,0**	1,4	1,8	1,9	**2,5**	1,3	1,6
Magazines	1,8	1,5	1,6	**2,4**	1,6	2,0	2,1	**2,8**	1,6	1,7
Books	1,9	1,9	1,7	**2,5**	1,8	1,6	1,9	**2,0**	1,3	1,5
Computers	2,9	2,7	2,9	**3,5**	2,7	3,0	3,2	**3,4**	2,6	2,8
Self estimation of competence in:										
... speaking	4,1	**4,3**	4,1	**4,3**	*3,9*	4,0	**4,3**	4,0	3,9	*3,8*
... listening	4,3	**4,4**	4,3	**4,4**	4,0	4,2	**4,4**	4,3	4,1	*3,9*
... writing	3,9	4,0	3,9	**4,1**	*3,7*	3,9	**4,1**	4,0	3,9	*3,7*
... reading	4,2	4,3	4,2	**4,4**	*4,0*	4,2	**4,4**	4,2	4,1	*4,0*
Other variables with regard to the English language:										
Like English	3,2	**3,4**	3,1	**3,4**	*2,9*	3,1	**3,4**	3,2	3,1	*2,7*
E. important	3,4	3,5	3,3	**3,6**	3,2	3,7	**3,8**	3,7	3,7	*3,4*
Meara test	62,6	61,3	63,5	**67,1**	57,7	53,3	**55,5**	54,8	52,5	*50,5*
Social background (proportion of selected clusters, in %):										
Boys	47,9	*40,6*	47,2	**53,0**	51,7	47,4	43,3	46,6	43,5	**61,3**
Highly educated parents	73,5	72,3	72,4	**76,8**	73,1	48,8	**56,0**	54,2	45,2	*40,9*
Vacations	67,6	69,4	70,3	*76,8*	*51,0*	66,9	**78,0**	69,5	61,8	*61,1*

Bold: highest value of all clusters; *italic*: lowest values of all clusters;
*) Different answer format (scale from 1=only German to 7=only English)

6.3.3 The Dutch sample

Cluster N1 is characterized by frequent contacts with English in the family and also by music. Differences observed in other characteristics shown elsewhere in Table 6.2 are not too substantial, but the general effects are statistically significant. (Procedure K-Means-Cluster, SPSS.) Cluster N1 has the highest proportion of girls, likes English, and estimates their own competence in speaking and listening English rather high. In cluster N2, English contact depends on music, while the other opportunities are just around the average. The main characteristic of the third Dutch cluster, N3, is the significantly higher frequency of contact with English in print media and computers; in addition, contacts via listening to music are numerous. In this cluster we also find the highest proportion of boys. The last cluster, N4, is characterized by generally low frequencies of contact with English; almost all proficiency criteria tend to the negative pole – be it the self-estimation or the vocabulary test. Further, this cluster does not seem to like English as much as the other clusters. This cluster is strikingly different from the other Dutch clusters with respect to whether they had ever been on vacations where they had to speak English; this was true for only one half of them, while more than two thirds of the total Dutch sample gave a positive answer to this question. In the case of cluster N3, the percent was even higher, with more than three quarters having used English while on a family vacation.

6.3.4 The German sample

In the German sample, cluster G1 has a particularly high frequency of contact with English within the family and attains the best proficiency results in all the variables involved here (self-assessment and vocabulary test). There are more girls than boys; parents are comparatively well educated; and opportunities to speak English during vacations are broad. The second German cluster, G2, is similar to the Dutch cluster N3 with respect to print and audiovisual media; however, unlike the N3 cluster, cluster G2 includes television and cinema. Cluster G3 claims to have frequent contacts with English language music and makes less frequent use of other sources. The last cluster, G4, is characterized by very few contacts with English, has the lowest measures for self-assessment and on the vocabulary test. Boys outnumber girls in this cluster, and parents' formal education is significantly lower than in the other clusters.

6.4   COPING WITH DIFFERENT KINDS OF SITUATIONS

So far it seems that the different kinds of media environments go along with general differences with regard to proficiency in English. Given this, our next step was to test the assumption that different contact patterns would shape different kinds of proficiency. To do this, factor analyses were run on the 34 items which asked respondents whether they believed they could cope with certain situations in English.

The Dutch sample. For the Dutch sample we got five factors: (1) the strong factor of *demanding everyday conversation*; (2) *simple everyday situations*; (3) *music and cinema*; (4) *easy listening*; and, (5) *writing* (Principal component analysis, varimax rotation, explained variance: 56.4%). Table 6.4 (upper part) shows the average factor scores for the different contact types as observed in the Dutch sample.

Cluster N4 has negative values in all dimensions, which is in line with the previous results presented for this cluster; it clearly has the weakest relationship to the English language in having just a few contacts with English. All indicators for proficiency are below the average, with almost no difference compared to the average values observed for cluster N2. This cluster, the largest of the Dutch sample, includes many contacts with English via music media, but very few contacts from other sources. In this respect it represents something like the "mainstream." Cluster N1 – those who have many contacts with English within their families – shows more positive values than all of the other clusters for the two dimensions that can be considered "culture oriented," namely, "music and cinema" and "complex writing" (e.g., translating song lyrics or writing a poem). This pattern of proficiency might be explained by the large number of girls within this cluster who live in families with high English proficiency (higher than in any other cluster), but whose parents have an educational level below the average.

Finally, cluster N3 has clear positive values for the main dimension: ability to take part in and to understand demanding conversations. This is quite in line with this cluster's attainment of the highest vocabulary test score as well as the highest self-estimates with regard to speaking, listening, writing and reading English. The contact pattern of this cluster recalls "educated" (as opposed to more mainstream) forms of media use: living in an environment with well-educated parents who often provide the opportunity to spend vacations in other countries, these young people are motivated to go beyond use of music media and to make contact with English by reading print media and accessing English language material on the computer in particular.

We wanted to compare the findings from the Dutch and the German samples, but knew that a direct comparison was not possible in the statistical sense since both the clusters and the dimensions have been calculated on the sub-sample level. Our solution is Table 6.3, which presents the data in a combined table rather than in two separate presentations.

Table 6.3
Coping with different kinds of situations in sub-groups with different media environments

	a) Netherlands					**b) Germany**				
	Total	**Cl. N1**	**Cl. N2**	**Cl. N3**	**Cl. N4**	**Total**	**Cl. G1**	**Cl. G2**	**Cl. G3**	**Cl. G4**
No. of cases	737	172	251	165	149	593	127	141	217	108
In % of total	100	23,3	34,1	22,4	20,2	100	21,4	23,8	36,6	18,2
a) Self estimation of coping different situations (The Netherlands):										
Dim. N1	.00	-.03	-.19	**.41**	-.09	Demanding everyday conversation				
Dim. N2	.00	.08	.09	-.01	-.24	Simple everyday situations				
Dim. N3	.00	**.13**	.00	.12	-.28	Music and cinema				
Dim. N4	.00	-.03	.09	.10	-.24	Easy listening				
Dim. N5	.00	**.22**	-.04	.06	-.27	Complex writing				
b) Self estimation of coping different situation (Germany):										
Dim. G1 Everyday conversation						.02	**.35**	.00	-.06	*-.21*
Dim. G2 Complex Communication						.02	.17	**.20**	*-.13*	-.11
Dim. G3 Formal situations						.01	**.17**	.03	*-.11*	.03
Dim. G4 Music and poems						.00	**.24**	.17	-.03	*-.44*
Dim. G5 Simple everyday situations						.00	-.06	.07	-.04	.07

Bold: highest value of all clusters; *italic*: lowest values of all clusters;
*) Different answer format.

For the German sample, in spite of some superficial differences, we find functionally analogous results (see Table 6.3, section b, "Germany"). Again, we find that the cluster G4 has very few contacts with English and low values for all proficiency indicators (self-assessments, vocabulary test). It also gets low values on three of the five dimensions of coping with different situations. These young people, mainly boys, are living in families with less-educated parents and few opportunities to learn English during vacations in other countries. G3 is another cluster with low figures on the coping dimensions, and corresponds to the Dutch cluster N2. As in the Netherlands, the young people whose only contact with English is via music media form the biggest cluster, and are below the average in their overall English proficiency. Cluster G2 (corresponding to N3) includes those young people who claim to have contacts with English in many different media. They perform better than clusters G3 and G4 on all coping dimensions; with regard to *complex communication* they are even better than G1. Contrary to the Dutch case, those in the print and audiovisual media cluster do not live in the most highly-educated families, but it is the case for cluster G1. The young people in this cluster do well on the vocabulary test and are at the top in self estimates of basic skills and of three of the five coping dimensions. Only with regard to the dimension which refers to the simplest situations are their results below average.

All in all, these exploratory analyses demonstrate that social background, media environment, and English proficiency are closely interrelated. The different clusters we have identified according to their patterns of mediated contacts with English also differ in their social background and in their particular competence in English.

6.5 MUSIC: A MEDIATED LINK TO ENGLISH LANGUAGE

Since music came out to be an important opportunity for contacts with the English language, we tried to differentiate patterns of music usage that were sensitive to the language of song lyrics. The survey had two questions about the importance of song lyrics: one asked about lyrics in one's own language (Dutch, French, or German, respectively), and the others about lyrics in English.

In the pilot phase of the study conducted in Germany (see Hasebrink, Berns & Skinner, 1997, p. 169), it was found that the average answers to these questions were quite similar: English texts were regarded as almost equally important as German texts. However, a joint analysis of the respective answers showed no correlation between them. For some young people, German texts were more important than English texts; for others, the opposite was true. This finding led us to assume that different attitudes towards song lyrics in either one's own language or in English are related to characteristics of language proficiency. In fact, results indicated a correlation between attitudes to song lyrics and specific kinds of language proficiency. These assumptions and findings from the pilot study were tested using data obtained from our surveys in Belgium, France, and the Netherlands, as well as the additional school groups surveyed in Germany.

In a first step we identified groups which differ in their attitude towards song lyrics in different languages. As shown in Chapter 4, lyrics in national languages are regarded as marginally more important (see Table 6.4) than English lyrics. However, there are differences among the research groups: although English lyrics are clearly more important than Dutch lyrics for the Nb group, the opposite is true for the G, and particularly the Bw and F groups. The Nn group and the Bf group show no difference for importance of the language of the song lyrics. Table 6.4 also shows the correlation between the respondents' answers to these two questions.

Table 6.4

Importance of song lyrics in English and in national languages

	Netherlands	Netherlands (bilingual)	Flanders	Wallonia	Germany	France	Total
N	782	325	199	117	615	144	2.182
Importance of English (mean)	2,45	2,73	2,75	2,55	2,54	2,37	2,55
Importance of national language (mean)	2,46	2,58	2,77	3,07	2,74	3,08	2,66
Correlation English / national language (r)	.33	.35	.21	.36	.29	.12	.29
1) All lyrics (rather) important (%)	28,9	40,9	48,2	49,6	35,3	33,3	35,7
2) Only English lyrics (rather) important (%)	16,8	20,6	18,1	6,0	13,7	6,3	15,3
3) Only lyrics in national language (rather) important (%)	18,7	12,9	19,6	29,1	26,3	49,3	22,6
4) All lyrics (rather) unimportant (%)	35,7	25,5	14,1	15,4	24,7	11,1	26,4

The clear positive correlation between the importance of national and English song lyrics (between .12 in the French and .36 in the Walloon sample) indicates an underlying dimension of general interest in lyrics. This dimension might be interpreted in terms of different patterns of education: young people growing up in a well-educated home environment are used to engaging with texts, and are motivated to comprehend these texts as well as song lyrics. However, the correlation between the importance of English and one's own language (.29 for the total sample) leaves quite a lot of variance. Thus, this general dimension does little to explain many of the responses in our sample. Thus, the importance of lyrics in the different languages is partly independent, as had been the case in the German pilot study. Thus, we can assume that specific forms of attitudes toward English lyrics might be linked to specific forms of English proficiency.

In order to test this assumption, an analysis was done that would define four groups of respondents who claim that:

Group 1)   all lyrics are (rather) important;
Group 2)   only English lyrics are (rather) important;
Group 3)   only national lyrics are (rather) important;
Group 4)   all lyrics are (rather) unimportant.

For the total sample, the group that considers all lyrics rather important (Group 1) is the largest, which indicates that in general young people do not just listen to the music alone, but also pay attention to the words, be they in English or the national language. This pattern of answers was observed particularly often in the two Belgian sub-samples. The smallest group is Group 2, with higher frequencies in the Dutch-speaking groups and very low frequencies in the French-speaking groups. These differences correspond to the general finding of higher English proficiency in the Netherlands and Flanders (see Chapter 4).

The third group, who regard song lyrics in their national language as more important than lyrics in English, presents the opposite pattern: nearly half of the French sub-sample belongs to this group, while in the Nb group, Group 3 is the smallest. The Dutch-speaking research samples most often regarded both English and national language lyrics as (rather) unimportant; these Group 4 differences are difficult to interpret.

At this point, we posited that these patterns of attitudes towards the languages of song lyrics should serve as an indicator for different media and language environments which correspond to different patterns of language proficiency. To test this, we focused on Group 2, consisting of those who regard English lyrics more important than lyrics in their own language, which we found particularly interesting.

Group 2 includes the highest proportion of young people who live in households with at least one language other than the national language (e.g., 44 % in the G group and 32 % in the Nb group). This was an important characteristic found in all the research samples involved. Based on this finding, we hypothesized that the young people in Group 2 are less centered on a national perspective than the other three groups. An indicator in favor of this hypothesis was found in the German sample, which was asked how much they liked German and English (as well as Dutch, French, and Turkish) and how much they liked people from Germany, England, America (as well as the Netherlands, France, and Turkey). Table 6.5 shows the results.

Table 6.5
Liking of languages and countries in groups with different patterns of attitudes to song lyrics (results for German sample only)

	Like German language	Like English language	Like German people	Like English people	Like American people
1) All lyrics (rather) important (%)	2,36	2,33	1,91	1,91	2,22
2) Only English lyrics (rather) important (%)	2,34	2,48	1,90	2,09	2,45
3) Only lyrics in national language (rather) important (%)	2,48	2,11	1,98	1,90	2,14
4) All lyrics (rather) unimportant (%)	2,47	2,09	2,04	1,89	2,10
	n. s.	p < .001	n. s.	n. s.	p < .01

Significances on the overall level only.

Only Group 2 likes the English language more than the German language. The same result holds for the question on how much they like people from the different countries. Young Germans generally seemed to like Americans more than Germans, but this finding is particularly clear for Group 2, which showed the least liking for Germans and the highest for Americans.

Further analyses of the social and educational background of the four groups indicate several differences. Respondents in Groups 2 and 4 are enrolled in lower forms of education. Also, the level of the parents' formal education is quite low in these groups. Yet, parents' and siblings' proficiency in English seems to be higher in Group 2.

As done with the different patterns of contact with English, we analyzed the differences between and among the four groups with regard to their attitudes towards and proficiency in English. Again, results are presented for the Dutch and German group because of the larger sample sizes (Table 6.6).

Table 6.6
Liking and proficiency of English in groups with different patterns of attitudes to song lyrics

	Netherlands					Germany				
	Total	**1)**	**2)**	**3)**	**4)**	**Total**	**1)**	**2)**	**3)**	**4)**
No. of cases	782	226	131	146	279	615	217	84	162	152
In % of total	100	28,9	16,8	18,7	35,7	100	35,3	13,7	26,3	24,7
Self estimation of competence in:										
...speaking	4,1	4,2	**4,3**	4,0	4,1	4,0	4,0	4,0	3,9	3,9
...listening	4,3	**4,5**	4,4	4,1	4,2	4,2	4,3	**4,3**	4,0	4,0
...writing	3,9	4,0	4,0	3,8	3,9	3,9	3,9	**4,1**	3,8	3,8
...reading	4,2	4,3	**4,4**	4,0	4,2	4,2	4,2	**4,4**	4,0	4,1
Other variables with regard to the English language:										
Like English	3,2	**3,4**	**3,4**	3,0	3,0	3,1	3,2	**3,4**	3,0	2,9
E. important	3,4	3,5	3,6	3,4	3,2	3,7	**3,8**	3,7	3,6	3,6
Meara test	62,1	**66,1**	60,2	62,9	59,5	53,2	**54,4**	49,1	**54,4**	52,5
Self estimation of coping different situations (The Netherlands):										
Dim. N1	.00	.14	.07	-.13	-.10					
Dim. N2	.00	.02	.11	-.09	-.01					
Dim. N3	.00	.16	**.30**	*-.40*	-.11					
Dim. N4	.00	.11	.03	.06	-.15					
Dim. N5	.00	.14	.10	-.15	-.09					
Self estimation of coping different situation (Germany):										
Dim. G1 Everyday conversation						Demanding everyday conversation				
Dim. G2 Complex Communication						Simple everyday situations				
Dim. G3 Formal situations						Music and cinema				
Dim. G4 Music and poems						Easy listening				
Dim. G5 Simple everyday situations						Complex writing				
Dim. G1						.01	**.13**	-.34	.02	.04
Dim. G2						.00	.08	**.31**	-.08	*-.19*
Dim. G3						.01	.03	**.20**	-.22	.05
Dim. G4						.00	.26	**.34**	-.18	*-.35*
Dim. G5						.00	-.05	**.13**	-.04	.04
Social background (proportion of selected groups, in %):										
Boys	47,0	40,4	**54,6**	49,7	47,3	47,4	40,9	40,5	46,6	**62,0**
Highly educated parents	73,9	**76,9**	70,6	71,9	74,0	48,8	48,1	41,8	**50,3**	45,5
Vacations	67,4	73,7	70,2	66,4	61,5	66,9	**70,4**	65,5	67,9	63,2

Bold: highest value of all groups; *italic*: lowest values of all groups.

The separate analyses for the Dutch and German sub-sample provide evidence that (1) differentiation between the four groups with respect to the relative importance of lyrics in either the national language or English is linked to differences in English proficiency; and, (2) the structure of the findings is surprisingly similar between the two countries.

This similarity is illustrated by the self-estimates of competence in speaking, listening, writing and reading English. Groups 1 and 2 are clearly better than the average in either country. These are the two groups that like English better and regard it as more important. However, Group 2 does not perform very well in the vocabulary test, while Groups 1 and 3 in both countries reached higher scores. Even though detailed comparison of the results among countries is not possible on the different dimensions of coping with concrete situations, one result becomes clear: either Group 1 or Group 2 gets the highest figures on all dimensions.

The results for Group 2 are even more remarkable since these young people's parents have the lowest level of formal education. This is an indicator that Group 2 falls outside a one-dimensional scale between "good" and "bad" English, which is often closely related to formal education. Instead, there are strong indicators that along the line between what might be called "formal" and "informal" situations there are different types of English proficiency. At least, there is a specific group of young people who are highly interested in music and English song lyrics and seem to like English very much and thus are quite proficient – as long as this judgment is based on their self-estimation, and not the vocabulary test on which they as a group got the lowest results of all groups. The only clear difference between the two samples is that Group 2 in the Netherlands is represented by more boys, whereas in Germany the opposite is true.

6.6   DISCUSSION

These findings support the assumption that different kinds of English proficiency are developed in the context of different media environments. The design of the study does not allow a definite answer to whether or not the media or the use of the media directly influences the level and the kind of proficiency in English. However, our findings clearly demonstrate that young people selectively choose the media which then build their media environment, which may differ quite substantially from group to group. These differences correspond to differences in English proficiency and underscore that proficiency may not be conceptualized as a one-dimensional construct. Instead, young people develop very specific and differentiated patterns of English proficiency.

We consider this finding one of the most relevant outcomes of our study because it has implications for Europeans' capability for intra-European communication. With English functioning as a lingua franca in Europe for the citizens of Europe, most parts of the European population will have to acquire at least a certain level of English. The particular level of proficiency and the particular communicative competence in English they acquire will depend on concrete needs, and in so far as needs are different and individualized to some degree, the specific kinds of English observed in different groups will differ substantially. Research on English acquisition and teaching will have to develop criteria of these dimensions of English proficiency, criteria that are more reliable and more easily interpreted for their meaning than the criteria offered by the self-assessment measures in this study.

Another important outcome was the surprising similarity across the four countries in many of the results produced by our analyses. We were particularly pleased with this outcome because it indicates that the administration of the surveys, in spite of differences in formats and in administrators, went well. But most important is our finding that there is a common ground of regularity in the lives of young people from different countries that provides a foundation upon which comparative researchers can build further studies.

Chapter 7

IN THE PRESENCE OF ENGLISH: A RESUME AFTER STEP ONE OF AN INTERNATIONAL STUDY

Uwe Hasebrink, Margie Berns, and Kees de Bot

7.1   INTRODUCTION

In the presence of English: This phrase refers to the starting point, to the common interest of a group of researchers from different countries and from different disciplines. Given the fact that English has become the lingua franca of Europe, and that English is by far the most important language of the global media, the common assumption is that young people are growing up in the presence of English and that English will be an important means of communication throughout their lives. But what kind of presence has the English language reached? What are the exact opportunities for young people in Europe to have contact with English? To what extent are there differences between countries, within countries, or between different social groups? What role do the media play? These were some of the questions that jointly motivated us to design an empirical research project.

This research has been innovative and therefore partly explorative in several aspects: (1) It combined questions and theoretical considerations from different disciplines – English language studies, sociolinguistics, communication and media studies, second language acquisition, and social psychology; (2) it followed an empirical approach in conducting standardized surveys covering topics as diverse as contacts with language, attitudes to languages, language proficiency, media use, and social background; and, (3) the research included international comparisons in trying to understand the impact of different cultural settings and language backgrounds.

This first approach to this rather challenging research design necessarily suffered from several restrictions which limit the range and the validity of the results: there has been no systematic experience in linking theoretical concepts from different disciplines; only a small number of European countries were involved; due to a lack of well-established scales and item formats, most parts of the questionnaire had to be constructed starting from almost zero; in comparative research, the problem of constructing different language versions of the questionnaire, which are supposed to measure "the same" in different cultural conditions, is always crucial; it was not possible to recruit really representative samples. However, while these shortcomings have to be kept in mind, the results of this research are an important step forward in the direction towards empirical, internationally comparative and interdisciplinary research on the role of English as a second language in the lives of young Europeans. In the following, first, we summarize results of our study which provide a clearer picture of what we understand as the "presence" of English. Next, we discuss consequences of this presence of English with regard to current social, cultural and political questions. Finally, we consider approaches for future research in this area which may help to contribute to the solution of these questions.

7.2   THE ENGLISH LANGUAGE AMONG EUROPEAN YOUTH: WHAT KIND OF PRESENCE?

7.2.1   Contact with English: Plurality of opportunities

At the very beginning of this study, the main hypothesis was that the English language seems to be "omnipresent" in the lives of young Europeans. This means that young people do not encounter this language in language classes at school only, but have plenty of opportunities where they can have contact with English. The results of our study clearly emphasize this basic notion. Beyond school, there are at least three important factors contributing to the presence of English: the media, personal networks, and intercultural communication as it is exercised during vacations and travels abroad.

7.2.1.1 School

Young people in Europe obviously have contact with the English language in school. Throughout Europe, English lessons at school are a common phenomenon. There is no doubt that English should be part of any level of general education. It seems to be a general trend in Europe to start earlier and to follow an approach to language teaching that regards English as an international language rather than a foreign language. Another trend is the move towards more bilingual schooling and more content-based language teaching. This is increasingly known as content and language integrated learning (CLIL), and refers to any dual-focused educational context in which an additional language - not usually the first language of the learners involved – is used as a medium in the teaching and learning of subjects other than language. Differences between countries are to be observed with regard to how far they have proceeded in these directions.

7.2.1.2 Media

The media provide a substantial amount of content in English. This is particularly true for music media, whether radio and pre-recorded or self-recorded (or downloaded) music. The vast majority of music listened to by young people in all of the countries studied is English language music. Since music plays a crucial role in the definition of youth cultures, and as such, forms one important element in the process of young people's identity construction, the English language is closely linked to the basic processes of defining cultural orientations and values.

In so far as other media are concerned, the European picture is less homogenous; different countries and linguistic environments provide different opportunities for English contacts via the media (see below). As a rule, transnational English language media - for example, CNN - are far behind national media in the respective native languages; pan-European channels, once a hope for enthusiasts of European integration, have failed because the question of language has proved to be a stumbling block. Even music channels like MTV Europe split up into different language versions in order to compete with national channels. This is a significant example for the strategy of "globalization" in which global players adapt global content to local audiences. Thus, besides the specific case of music, popular mass media do not provide many opportunities for contact with English.

If we take the computer and the internet as new media, these new communication options lead to a substantial change in the presence of English. Next to music media, computers were the second important media source of English. As a consequence of (1) the globalized new technology slang or jargon which is mainly Anglo-American, (2) international software tools with their English help functions and handbooks, and, (3) the main feature of the internet to allow for getting information from anywhere in the world within seconds, online communication has become a powerful platform for a globalized use of English.

7.2.1.3 Personal networks

Several factors of social change cause a trend towards increasing contacts with English, even in personal networks. European societies are facing a further increase of migration; "multi-cultural society" is the common notion for today's situation, which includes many opportunities for contact with different cultures and languages. Thus, we find multi-lingual families, multi-lingual neighborhoods, multi-lingual school classes and so on.

7.2.1.4 Intercultural communication

The communicative links between different countries and cultures are growing tighter and tighter. The numbers of people traveling abroad during vacations are increasing, although the consequences of the terrorist attack of September 11, 2001 interrupted this trend for a while. Various institutions, with the European Commission and many NGOs among them, encourage young people to take part in international exchange programs. Mobility as such is one of the aims of the European Union's policies. As a consequence, the probability of meeting people from other countries and cultures, and therefore the need to communicate in English, is growing. With regard to these situations of interpersonal contacts, the lingua franca character of English in Europe is quite obvious: Germans use English to communicate with Spanish or French people during their vacations in Spain or France.

7.2.2 The new quality of the presence of English

The foregoing paragraphs have shown that all the factors influencing contacts with English indicate a strong trend towards an increase in the presence of English. This trend should not be understood in quantitative terms only; it is also a qualitative change in the kind of presence. Different opportunities to have contact with English are linked with different socio-linguistic functions. With each additional opportunity to use English its functionality increases: the language develops from a rather uni-dimensional tool - for example, to take part in international pop music or to solve classical tasks in English lessons at school - to a multi-dimensional means of expression and communication which is linked to the professional sphere as well as the private sphere, to globalized mass media entertainment as well as private communication.

One consequence of this multi-optional presence of English is that different groups will create their personal language environments according to their individual needs and capacities. And, as has been argued in Chapter 6, different language and media environments shape different kinds of English proficiency. These differences underscore assertion that proficiency cannot be conceptualized as a one-dimensional construct. Instead, young people develop very specific and differentiated patterns of English proficiency.

Patterns of availability of English substantially differ between countries. Although the selection of countries involved in the present study was quite limited, one important difference became quite clear: the difference between bigger and smaller language markets. The Dutch speaking regions – and, as other studies indicate, the Nordic countries as well – provide many more opportunities for contact with English than the French- or German-speaking regions – and, as other studies indicate, we can make the same argument for Italy or Spain. English proficiency of the Dutch population is far higher, thus parents are more likely to be able to speak English; English lessons start earlier, and there are more English classes; there is no dubbing of English or American content in cinema or television, thus Dutch children have far more opportunities to listen to English and, by means of subtitles, to learn to understand the language.

As a consequence, indicators of English proficiency are generally higher in Dutch-speaking regions than they are in Germany or France. This does not necessarily mean that knowing English is regarded as less important in the latter countries; at least in Germany, young people believe that speaking and understanding English will be a very important tool for their professional lives in particular. This dissociation between low performance and high (instrumental) interest might be interpreted as follows: Whereas in Germany English is regarded as a necessary professional qualification which has to be learned like other formal qualifications, young people in the Netherlands regard English as one means to express themselves and their cultural orientation. It has to be emphasized that there is no "either – or" relation between these two functions, but with regard to the relative weight of these two aspects young people in the countries we have investigated in this study show clear differences which can be explained by different economic, political and cultural conditions in the respective countries.

7.3 THE PRESENCE OF ENGLISH: WHAT KIND OF CONSEQUENCES?

7.3.1 The presence of English and its consequences for language teaching

The omnipresence of English in the lives of young people and the diversity of functions this language serves them has substantial consequences for language teaching. As has been shown very clearly in this study, school is but one source of contact with English – and at least for some groups not the most important one. Thus, the type of English the students acquire is only partly controlled by the school. The variety of English set up as the classroom model and the one that teachers and textbooks present in lessons is likely to differ from that learned by the pupils. Since school is just one among many sources of contact with English, the English used by learners is likely to be a mix based on English learned at school as well as English from lyrics, computer games, TV programs, and films. It is unlikely that this will lead to one coherent and consistent variety, and the consequences for teaching English range from the expectations for the levels of proficiency to be achieved, the nature of the communicative competence to be developed, standards for assessment, and reconsideration of the role of the native speaker.

Language teacher education and English-language studies are also implicated in changes in the classroom and its linguistic norms. Not the least of these is attention to the interaction between motivation and the linguistic attitudes of teachers as well as learners. As shown, seeking membership in a particular cultural group, in this case, youth culture, relates not only to the desire to learn English, but to the subset of the language that is learned and the norms of its use as well. Learners' remolding of English through participation in interaction to suit their goals and needs is as essential as the acquisition of its structure.

7.3.2   The presence of English and its consequences for the workplace

The presence of English in the workplace has consequences for employers and employees alike with respect to productivity and profit for the former and employability and upward mobility for the latter. The adoption of English for communication in the office or on the shop floor, if it reflects genuine communicative needs, can affect the workforce differentially depending upon individuals' level of proficiency. For instance, do those who use it feel more highly valued or distinguished in any way? In multilingual work settings, misunderstandings can have serious consequences, which can result from the use of English or can be the very motivation for adopting English.

If English is adopted, important considerations are whether or not the workforce has the capacity to determine linguistic practices and to assert an identity. If it feels it necessary to accept the use of English in their field or specialty, they still might resist accepting the power relationships imposed by management's decision for English. The consequences of such choices for the language of the country from which the company originates remain open. Similarly, little is known about language practices in small and medium enterprises which have gone international. Studies in this sector have been carried out with a view to providing guidance to companies. As these have focused on the use of language for export (Hagen, 1999), they represent only the tip of the iceberg of linguistic practices in business and industry.

7.3.3. The presence of English and its role for the development of European public spheres

The European process of integration requires acceptance and support from the population, it requires active participation. As a pre-condition for this, Europe needs the evolution of a European public sphere, which means a broad public discourse on European affairs which allows for the exchange of conflicting views and arguments or even for building consensus. In this respect the European process does not seem to be favorably disposed. What is often discussed as a deficit in democracy on the European level might be interpreted as a deficit in communication on the European level – and this deficit is closely linked to language barriers.

There are different models of European public spheres, each referring to a specific role of the English language: a pan-European language, a language for field and topic specialists, or as lingua franca among continental Europeans.

The most ambitious is that of a pan-European public sphere, which is built by pan-European media, targeted at a trans-national audience. This model needs a common language, because all approaches to provide different language versions, for example, Euronews, would run counter to the aim of a joint audience. As all former experiences of pan-European media offers have shown, this understanding of a European public sphere does not at all reflect the actual situation. With the significant exception of music there is no European market for mass media content in any single language. Our results, referring to young people, underline this general experience: Young people in Europe use national media and they prefer media in their own language – with the exception of music, where songs with English lyrics are clearly preferred to songs in their national language. However, this finding cannot be interpreted as an indicator for English serving as a pan-European language; it rather points to the popularity and modern image of globalized pop music, thus the "sound of English" might be more important than the language as a means for communication.

The second – less ambitious, but more realistic – understanding of European public spheres might be called a model of segmented thematic spheres. This model emphasises that within Europe plenty of communication networks have been evolved with segmented subparts, which focus on particular topics or issues, for example, scientific communities, politicians, NGOs. Within these networks one can state that English clearly has the status of a lingua franca – most of these groups use English for communication in professional publications or official documents, at professional meetings or in research labs. By definition the mass media do not play a substantial role for these spheres because the respective topics are by far too sophisticated. It is the internet and the English language that provide the most appropriate form of communication for such public spheres. And in them, it is likely that quite different kinds of English will evolve, which serve the primary function of the respective group in their domain of use. According to our research young people in Europe actually use English for sharing their views with specific target groups throughout Europe and beyond. The internet and the English language – together they provide the basis for trans-national communication on specific areas of interest.

The third understanding of European public spheres refers to the level of individual behavior, of personal contacts with people from other European countries. With English functioning as a lingua franca in Europe for the citizens of Europe, most parts of the European population will have to acquire at least a certain level of English in order to organize their personal life. And this applies not only to the teenagers from different European countries who already use English as a means of mutual understanding; everyone will be a user of English to some degree – for schooling and training, for travel and employment, for recreational and cultural activities – both within and beyond their local environment. The particular level of proficiency and the particular communicative competence in English they acquire will depend on concrete needs, and in so far as needs are different and individualized to some degree, the specific kinds of English to be observed will differ substantially. As seen with the participants in this study, young people develop very specific and differentiated patterns of English proficiency.

The last two models of European public spheres and the respective role of English can be interpreted as a strong argument against the well-known concern that English as a lingua franca could serve as a factor of Anglo-American hegemony and cultural homogenization. According to these models, English would rather serve as the minimal communicative condition which would allow people from different countries and cultures to develop their specific way to communicate. The result of this process might even be that British or American partners would have the biggest problems in understanding – since the actual language used is not the English they know.

Additionally, these two models refer to the establishment – through English – of additional identities. English serves as a marker of a social identity, of group relations, but does not replace the identities established in the first language or the language of the home. Instead, the new identity is drawn from what English offers as a linguistic and cultural resource, one that individuals have at their disposal to communicate effectively in the lingua franca context that is Europe. As a close look at the media environments created by the young people in this study demonstrated, these additional identities are not necessarily circumscribed by national boundaries or by language communities.

7.3.4 The presence of English as an object for future research

As stated earlier, this international study was an explorative step towards an interdisciplinary, empirical and internationally comparative approach to the phenomenon of English as a second language in Europe. It is evident that this first step could not solve all the problems associated with and stemming from this kind of research and that many more questions were raised than were answered.

In face of the results, since we first began this project, we have become even more convinced than at the beginning that this kind of research is a route to a better understanding of the role of English as a means of communication in Europe. We are likewise convinced that increased understanding of the role of English is needed in order to provide more systematic and empirically grounded evidence and orientation for decision makers in the process of European integration, in school politics, and in the media. This conviction is grounded in realization of the long term effect and considerable social consequences of the interaction, as described in this project, between young people's use of media, attitudes toward languages and cultures, and proficiency in and actual use of English.

References

A.C.C. (1829). Corruptions of the English language. *Gentleman's Magazine* 99 (February): 121-123.

Ammon, U. (1994). The present dominance of English in Europe. With an outlook on possible solutions to the European language problems. *Sociolinguistica.* 8, 1-14.

Ammon, U. (1998). *Ist Deutsch noch internationale Wissenschaftssprache? Englisch auch für die Lehre an den deutschsprachigen Hochschulen* [Is German still the international language of science? English for instruction at German universities too]. Berlin/New York: de Gruyter.

Ammon, U. (2000). Towards more fairness in international English: linguistic rights on non-native speakers? In R. Phillipson (Ed.), *Rights to language: equity, power, and education* (pp. 111-116). Mahwah, NJ: Lawrence Erlbaum Associates.

Ammon, U. (Ed.) (2001). *Dominance of English as a language of science.* Berlin: Mouton de Gruyter.

Ammon, U. and McConnell, G. (2002). *English as an academic language in Europe: A survey of its use in teaching.*

Bachman, L. F. & Savignon, S.J. (1986). The evaluation of communicative language proficiency: A critique of the ACTFL oral interview. *Modern Language Journal* 70, 380-390.

Baetens-Beardsmore, H. (1997). Manipulating the variables in bilingual education (or: You can't beat them all). *Report on the conference on European networks in bilingual education.* Alkmaar, The Netherlands: European platform for Dutch education 8-15.

Bailey, R. W. (1991). *Images of English: A cultural history of the language.* Ann Arbor: University of Michigan Press.

Bandura, A. & Walters, R. H. (1963). *Social learning and personality development.* New York: Holt, Rinehart, and Winston.

Beheydt, L. (1996). *Kenterende culturele identiteit.* Amsterdam: University of Amsterdam.

Berlamont, J. (2002, May 23). Hoger onderwijs in het Engels moet kunnen [Higher education in English must be possible]. *De Standaard*, 10.

Berns, M. (1990). *Contexts of competence: Social and cultural considerations in communicative language teaching.* New York: Plenum Press.

Berns, M. (1995a). English in Europe: Whose language, which culture? *International Journal of Applied Linguistics* 5(1), 21-32.

Berns, M. (1995b). English in the European Union. *English Today* 11(3), 3-11.

Biersack, W., Dostal, W., Parmentier, K., Plicht, H., & Troll, L. (1988-89) *Arbeitssituation, Tätigkeitsprofil und Qualifikationsstruktur von Personengruppen des Arbeitsmarktes* [The employment situation, job profile and qualification structure of groups on the labor market]. BIBB/IAB- Erhebung. Retreived from http://www.iab.de/iab/publikationen/inh248.htm

Bollag, B. (September 8, 2000). The new Latin: English dominates in academe. *Chronicle of Higher Education,* A73.

Bailey, R. W. (1991). *Images of English: A cultural history of the language.* Ann Arbor: University of Michigan Press.

The Bulletin. (2005). Brussels: Ackroyd Publications.

Byram, M. (1996). Language teaching and European integration – Teaching culture for a *lingua franca.* In Sebbage, S. T. & T., (Eds.), *Languages through culture – Culture through languages* (pp. 9-14). Hamburg: T+S Team/Sebbage.

Carli, A. & Calaresu, E. (2003). Le lingue della comunicazione scientifica. La produzione e la diffusione del sapere specialistico in Italia [The language of scientific communication. The production and diffusion of specialist knowledge in Italy]. *Ecologia Linguistica, Atti del XXXVI° Congresso Internazionale di Studi della Società Linguistica Italiana.* A. Valentini, P. Molinelli, P. Cuzzolin and G. Bernini. Rome: Bolatti Boringhieri/Bulzoni: 27-74.

Carstensen, B. (1980). Euro-English. *Linguistics across historical and geographical boundaries. In honor of Jacek Fisiak on the occasion of his fiftieth birthday.* D. Kastovky, & Szedek, A. (Eds.). (pp. 827-834). Berlin: Mouton de Gruyter.

Cenoz, J. & Jessner, U., (Eds). (2000). *English in Europe: The acquisition of a third language.* Bilingual Education and Bilingualism. Clevedon, England: Multilingual Matters.

Clark, J. & Jorden, E. H. (1984). *A study of language attrition in former US students of Japanese and implications for design of curriculum and teaching materials.* Washington, DC: Center for Applied Linguistics.

Clement, R., & Gardner, R., & Smythe, P. (1977a). Motivational variables in second language acquisition: a study of francophones learning English. *Canadian Journal of Behaviorial Science* 9, 123-133.

Clement, R., & Gardner, R., & Smythe, P. (1977b). Inter-ethnic contact: Attitudinal consequences. *Canadian Journal of Behaviorial Science* 9, 205-215.

Confederation of EU Rectors' Conferences & Association of European Universities. (2001). Bologna Declaration on the European Space for Higher Education: An explanation. (2000). Retrieved October 22, 2003 from http://europa.eu.int/comm/education/policies/educ/bologna/bologna.pdf.

Coppieters 't Wallant, B. (1997). *Les besoins linguistiques dans les entreprises* [Language needs in business]. Université Catholique de Louvain, Belgium: Institut d'Administration et de Gestion.

Crystal, D. (1985). How many millions? The statistics of English today. *English Today* 1, 7-9.

Crystal, D. (1997). *Cambridge encyclopedia of language.* Cambridge: Cambridge University Press.

Crystal, D. (1997). *English as a global language.* Cambridge: Cambridge University Press.

DAAD (2003). Study and research in Germany. Retrieved October 22, 2003 from http://www.daad.de/deutschland/en/2.2.4.html.

de Bens, E. (2000). The Belgian media landscape. Retrieved October 3, 2003 from: http://www.ejc.nl/jr/emland/belgium.html.

de Bens, E. & Ross, G. (2002). *Medien in Belgien. Internationales Handbuch Medien 2002/2003*. [Media in Belgium. International Handbook of Media 2002/2003]. Hans-Bredow-Institut. Baden-Baden, Germany: Nomos: 206-222.

de Bot, K., Jagt, J., Janssen, H., Kessels, E. & Schils, E. (1986). Foreign television and language maintenance. *Second Language Research* 2(1), 72-82.

de Bot, K. & Weltens, B. (1997). Multilingualism in the Netherlands? In T. Bongaerts & K. de Bot (Eds.). *Perspectives on foreign language policy. Studies in honour of Theo van Els* (pp. 143-156). Amsterdam: John Benjamins.

de Mooij, M. (1994). *Advertising worldwide*. New York: Prentice Hall.

de Swaan, A. (1991). Nederlands kans in taal en cultuur [Dutch risk in language and culture]. *Ons Erfdeel* 34(4), 511-18.

Delbeke, L. (August 8, 2002). Engels in het hoger onderwijs. Een 'stille krimp van het Nederlands' of een 'stille schreeuw om (taal)vrijheid'? [English in higher education. A silent shrinking of Dutch or a silent scream for (language) freedom?]. *Campuskrant, Universiteit Leuven, 2.*

Denis, M.S. (1999). Etude, en Communauté française de Belgique, de l'importance des langues, de l'allemand en particulier, dans le processus de recrutement et de sélection des entreprises [Study on the French Community in Belgium, on the importance of languages, of German in particular, and on recruitment and selection procedures in companies]. Université Catholique de Louvain, Belgium: Institut d'Administration et de Gestion.

Denison, N. (1981). English in Europe, with particular reference to the German-speaking area. In W. Poeckl (Ed.). *Europäische Mehrsprachigkeit* [European multilingualism] (pp. 3-18). Tübingen: Max Niemeyer.

Devreese, J. (2002, May 28). Kwaliteit drijft boven, ook in het Nederlands (Quality prevails, also in Dutch). *De Standaard, 7.*

d'Haenens, L. (2001). Old and new media: Access and ownership in the home. In S. Livingstone & M. Bovill (Eds.). *Children and their changing media environment. A European comparative study.* (pp. 53-84). New York: Erlbaum.

Dickson, P. & Cumming, A. (Eds.) (1996). *Profiles of language education in 25 countries.* Slough, UK: National Foundation for Educational Research.

DGLF (Délégation générale à la langue française), (1998). *Rapport 1998.* Paris: La Documentation Française.

D'ydevalle, G. & Pavakanun, U. (1997). Could enjoying a movie lead to language acquisition. In P. Winterhoff-Spurk & T.H.A. van der Voort (Eds.). *New horizons in media psychology* (pp. 145-155). Opladen, Germany: Westdeutscher Verlag.

Ellis, R. (1986). *Understanding second language acquisition.* Oxford: Oxford University Press.

Etiemble, R. (1968). *Parlez-Vous Franglais?* [Do you speak Franglais?] Paris: Gallimard.

European Audiovisual Observatory (2001). *Focus 2001. World film market trend.* Strasbourg: Cannes Market.

European-Central-Bank (1999). *The euro banknotes and coins.* Frankfurt: European Central Bank.

European Commission. (1996). *Eurobarometer 44 (Standard).* Brussels: European Commission.

European Commission. (1997). *Eurobarometer 47 (Standard).* Brussels: European Commission.

European Commission. (1998). *Eurobarometer 47.1.* Brussels: European Commission.

European Commission. (1999). *Eurobarometer 50.* Brussels, European Commission.

European Commission. (2000). *Key data on education in Europe 1999/2000.* Brussels: European Commission.

European Commission. (2001a). *Eurobarometer 54.1 (Special). Europeans and languages.* Brussels: European Commission.

European Commission. (2001b). *Eurobarometer 55.1. (Special). The young Europeans.* Brussels: European Commission.

European Commission. (2001, October). *Eurobarometer 55. (Standard).* Brussels: European Commission.

European Commission. (2002). *Eurobarometer 56. Public Opinion in the European Union.* Brussels: Author.

European Commission. (2003). *Eurobarometer -2003.1. Public Opinion in the Candidate Countries.* Brussels: Author.

European Commission. (2005). *Eurobarometer 243, wave 64.3. Europeans and their languages.* Brussels: Author.

European Commission. (2002). *Key data on education in Europe, 2002.* Brussels: Author.

European Commission. (2002). *A new impetus for European youth. European Commission white paper.* Luxembourg: Author.

European Commission. (n.d.). *European report on quality of school education: Sixteen quality indicators.* Brussels: Author.

European Commission/Institut-der-deutschen-wirtschaft. (2001, March) . *Fonds, 3,* 6.

Eurostat. (1997). *Report.* Brussels: European Commission.

Eurydice. (1997). *Secondary education in the European Union: Structures, organisation and administration.* Brussels: Author.

Eurydice. (2001). *Foreign language teaching in schools in Europe.* Brussels: Author.

Eurydice. (2002). *Key data on education in Europe - 2002 edition.* Brussels: Author.

Eurydice. (2004). *Key data on information and communication technology in schools in Europe – 2004 edition.* Brussels: Author.

Eurydice. (2005). *Key data on teaching languages at schools in Europe – 2005 edition.* Brussels: Author.

Firth, J. R. (1957). *Papers in linguistics 1934 - 1951.* Oxford: Oxford University Press.

Fishman, J. A. (1998-99). The new linguistic order. *Foreign Policy* (Winter), 26-40.

Flaitz, J. (1988). *The ideology of English: French perceptions of English as a world language.* Berlin: Mouton de Gruyter.

Gardner, R. (1985). *Social psychology and second language learning: The role of attitude and motivation.* London: Edward Arnold.

Gardner, R. & Lambert, W. (1972). *Attitudes and motivation in second-language learning.* Rowley, MA: Newbury House.

Gardner, R. & McIntyre, P.D. (1993). A student's contribution to second language learning. Part II: Affective variables. *Language Teaching* 26, 1-11.

Garza, T.J. (1991). Evaluating the use of captioned video materials in advanced foreign language learning. *Foreign Language Annals*, 24, 239-258.

Gawlitta, L. (2001). *Akzeptanz englischsprachiger Werbeslogans. "Let's make things better"* [Acceptance of English language advertising slogans. "Let's make this better"]. Paderborn, Germany: IFB Verlag.

Gerbner, G. (1972). Violence in television drama: Trends and symbolic functions. In G. Comstock & E. Rubenstein (Eds.), *Television and social behavior, Vol. 1: Media Content and control.* Washington, DC: US Government Printing Office.

Gerritsen, M. (1995). "English" advertisements in the Netherlands, Germany, France, Italy, and Spain. In B. Machova & S. Kubatova (Eds.), *Sietar Europa 1995 Proceedings: Uniqueness in unity: The significance of cultural identity in European cooperation* (pp. 324-341).

Gerritsen, M., Korzilium, H., van Meurs, F & Gijsbers, I. (1999). Engels in commercials op de Nederlandse televisie. Frequentie, uitspraak, attitude en begrip [English in commercials on Dutch television: frequently used, attitudes and understanding]. *Tijdschrift voor Communicatiewetenschap* 27(2), 167-186.

Gnutzmann, C. (Ed.). (1999). *Teaching and learning English as a global language: native and non-native perspectives.* Tübingen: Stauffenberg Verlag.

Goethals, M. (1997). English in Flanders (Belgium). *World Englishes* 16(1), 105-114.

Graddol, D. (1997). *The future of English? A guide to forecasting the popularity of the English language in the 21st century.* London: British Council.

Graddol, D. (2001). The future of English as a European lingua franca. *The European English Messenger* (2): 47-55.

Grendel, M. (1993). *Verlies en herstel van lexicale kennis* [The loss and reconstruction of lexical knowledge]. Unpublished doctoral dissertation, University of Nijmegen, Nijmegen, The Netherlands.

Hagen, S. (1994). Language policy and planning for business in Great Britain. In R.D. Lambert (Ed.). *Language planning round the world: Contexts and systematic change* (pp. 111-130). Washington, DC: National Foreign Language Council.

Hagen, S. (Ed.). (1999). *Business communication across borders: A study of language use and practice in European companies.* London: Languages National Training Organisation.

Halliday, M. (1975). *Learning how to mean: Explorations in the development of language.* London: Edward Arnold.

Halliday, M. A. K. (1978). *Language as social semiotic.* London: Edward Arnold.

Hasebrink, U. (1997). In search of patterns of individual media use. In U. Carlsson (Ed.). *Beyond media uses and effects* (pp. 99-112). Goteborg, Sweden: Nordicom.

Hasebrink, U. (2001). Englisch als europäische Mediensprache. Empirische Annäherungen an eine interdisziplinäre Frage [English as the langauge of European media: Empirical approaches to an interdisciplinary question]. In D. Mohn, D. Ross & M. Tjarks-Sobhani (Eds.) *Mediensprache und Medienlinguistik. Festschrift für Jorg Hennig* (pp. 156-174). Frankfurt/Main: Peter Lang.

Hasebrink, U. (2003). Radio. In H.-O. Hügel (Ed.). *Handbuch populäre Kultur.* (pp. 359-365). Stuttgart/Weimar, Germany: Verlag J.B. Metzler.

Hasebrink, U., Berns, M. & Skinner, E. (1997). The English language within the media worlds of European youth. In P. Winterhoff-Spurk & T.H.A. van der Voort (Eds.). *New horizons in media psychology* (pp. 156-174). Opladen, Germany: Westdeutscher Verlag.

Hasebrink, U. & Herzog, A. (2002). Mediennutzung im internationalen Vergleich [International comparison of media use]. *Internationales Handbuch Medien 2002/2003*. Baden-Baden: Hans-Bredow-Institut. 109-129.

Hawkins, R. P., Reynolds, N. & Pingree, S. (1991). In search of viewing styles. *Journal of Broadcasting and Electronic Media* 35(3), 375-383.

Hofstede, G. (1980). *Culture's consequences: International differences in work-related values.* Beverly Hills: Sage Publications.

Hofstede, G. (1991). *Cultures and organizations.* New York: McGraw-Hill International.

Hofstede, G. (1996). The nation-state as a source of common mental programming: Similarities and differences across Eastern and Western Europe. In **S. Gustavsson & L. Lewin (Eds.).** *The future of the nation state: Essays on cultural pluralism and political integration* (19-48). London & New York/ Stockholm, Sweden: Routledge/Nerenius & Santérus Publishers.

Huibregtse, I. (2001). Effecten en Didactiek van tweetalig voortgezet onderwijs in Nederland [Effects and didactics of bilingual secondary education in the Netherlands]. Unpublished doctoral dissertation, University of Utrecht, Utrecht, The Netherlands.

Huibregste, I., Admiraal, W. & Meara, P. (2002). Scores on a yes-no vocabulary test: Correction for guessing and response style. *Language Testing* 19(3), 227-245.

Hymes, D. (1972). Competence and performance in linguistic theory. In R. Huxley & E. Ingram (Eds.). *Language acquisition: models and methods* (pp. 3-28). London: Academic Press.

Ingleton, R. D. (1994). *Mission incomprehensible.* Clevedon, England: Multilingual Matters.

Janssen, M., Janssen-van Dieten, A., & Evers, R. (1997). *Evaluatie Engels in het Voortgezet Onderwijs: Een Vooronderzoek Bij Twee Scholen* [Evaluation of English in secondary education: A preliminary investigation in two schools]. Nijmegen, The Netherlands: Department of Applied Linguistics, University of Nijmegen.

Johnson, E. (2000). Talking across frontiers. Paper Presented at the International Conference on European Cross Border Cooperation: Lessons for and from Ireland. Queen's University Belfast.

Johnsson-Smaragdi, U. (2001). Media use styles among the young. In S. Livingstone & M. Bovill (Eds.). *Children and their changing media environment: A European comparative study* (pp. 113-139). Mahwah, N.J: Lawrence Erlbaum Associates.

Johnsson-Smaragdi, U., d'Haenens, L., Krotz, F., & Hasebrink, U. (1998). Patterns of old and new media use among young people in Flanders, Germany and Sweden. *European Journal of Communication* 13(4), 479-501.

Jöreskog, K. G. & Sörbom, D. (1981). *LISREL 8.13.* Hillsdale, NJ: Lawrence Erlbaum Associates.

Kachru, B. B. (1976). Indian English: A sociolinguistic profile of a transplanted language. In *Dimensions of bilingualism.* Special issue of *Studies in Language Learning* 1(2), 79-108.

Kachru, B. B. (1983). *The Indianization of English: The English language in India.* Oxford: Oxford University Press.

Kachru, B. B. (1985). Standards, codification and sociolinguistic realism: the English language in the outer circle. In R. Quirk & H.G. Widdowson (Eds.). *English in the world: Teaching and learning the languages and literatures* (pp. 11-30). Cambridge: Cambridge University Press.

Kachru, B. B. (1997). World Englishes 2000: resources for research and teaching. In L.E. Smith & M.L. Forman (Eds.). *Literary studies east and west: World Englishes 2000* (pp. 209-251). Honolulu: University of Hawai'i Press.

Königs, F. G. (1999). To know English or not to know English: Some thoughts on the hegemony of English from a methodological point of view, with special reference to German as a foreign language. In C. Gnutzmann (Ed.). *Teaching and learning English as a global language: Native and non-native perspectives* (pp. 247-258). Tübingen: Stauffenburg Verlag.

Krotz, F. & Hasebrink, U. (1998). The analysis of people meter data: individual patterns of viewing behavior and viewers' cultural background. *Communication* 23(2), 151-174.

Lambert, R. D. (Ed.). (1994). *Language planning around the world: Contexts and systematic change.* Washington, DC: National Foreign Language Council.

Lammert, N. (2001). Mehr Deutsch in der deutschen Sprache. [More German in the German language.] *FOCUS* 17, 98.

Lantolf, J. P. (2000). Introducing sociocultural theory. In J.P. Lantolf (Ed.). *Sociocultural theory and second language acquisition* (pp. 1-26). Oxford: Oxford University Press.

Livingstone, S. & Bovill, M. (Eds.). (2001). *Children and their changing media environment: A European comparative study.* Mahwah, N.J.: Lawrence Erlbaum Associates.

Marsh, D., Marsland, B. & Maljers, A. (1998). Future scenarios in content and language integrated learning. Jyväskylä, Finland: University of Jyväskylä/The Hague: European Platform for Dutch Education.

Martin, E. (2002a). Cultural images and different varieties of English in French television commercials. *English Today 72* 18(4), 8-20.

Martin, E. (2002b). Mixing English in French advertising. *World Englishes* 21(3), 375-402.

Martin, E. & Hilgendorf, S. (2001). English in Advertising: Update from France and Germany. In E. Thumboo (Ed.). *The three circles of English.* (pp. 217-240). Singapore: Uni Press/National University of Singapore.

MacWilliam, I. (1986). Video and language comprehension. *ELT Journal* 40/42, 131-135.

McArthur, T. (1998). *The English languages.* Cambridge: Cambridge University Press.

Meara, P. (1992). *EFL vocabulary tests.* University of Wales, Swansea: Centre for Applied Language Studies.

Meara, P. & Buxton, B. (1987). An alternative to multiple choice vocabulary tests. *Language Testing* 4(2), 142-154.

Meara, P. M. & Jones, G. (1988). Vocabulary size as a placement indicator. *Applied linguistics in society.* P. Grunwell (Ed.). London: CILT/National Centre for Languages, 80-87.

Meara, P. M. & Jones, G. (1990). *The Eurocentres 10K vocabulary size test.* Zurich: Eurocentres Learning Service.

Meskill, C. (1998). Commercial television and the limited English proficient child: Implications for naturalistic and academic linguistic development. In K. Swan, R. Muffaletto, C. Meskill & D. Steven (Eds.). *Social learning from broadcast television* (pp. 61-85).Cresskill, NJ: Hampton Press.

Ministere-de-L'education-nationale. (2000). Rapport. Paris: Ministere de L'education nationale.

Mitchell, R., & Myles, F. (1998). *Second language learning theories.* London, Arnold.

Motz, M., Ed. (2005). *Englisch oder Deutsch internationalen studiengängen?* Frankfurt am Main, Peter Lang.

Mueller, G. (1980). Visual contextual cues and listening comprehension: An experiment. *Modern Language Journal*, 64(3), 335-340.

Nickerson, C. (2000). *Playing the corporate language game. An investigation of the genres and discourse strategies in English used by Dutch writers working in multinational corporations* (vol. 15). Amsterdam-Atlanta: Rodopi.

Oreja, M. (Ed.). (1998). *The digital age: European audiovisual policy. Report from the High Level Group on Audiovisual Policy.* Brussels: European Commission.

Otto, J. (2000, June 15). Hüpfen und tauchen: wie grundschüler Englisch und Französisch lernen. *Die Zeit,* p. 67.

Oud-de Glas, M. (1997). The difficulty of Spanish for Dutch learners. In T. Bongaerts and K. d. Bot (Eds.). *Perspectives on foreign-language policy.* (pp 41-54). Philadelphia/Amsterdam: John Benjamins.

Palmer, F. R. (1968). *Selected papers of J. R. Firth 1952 - 1959.* Bloomington, IN: University of Indiana Press.

Parker, R. (1995). *Mixed signals: the prospects for global television news.* New York: Twentieth Century Fund Press.

Pennycook, A. (1994). *The cultural politics of English as an international language.* Harlow, England: Longman.

Phillipson, R. (1992). *Linguistic imperialism.* Oxford: Oxford University Press.

Piepho, H.-E. (1988). Englisch als lingua franca in Europa: ein Appell zur didaktischen Bescheidenheit an das Fach Englisch und seine Vertreter [English as a European lingua franca: an appeal for pedagogical modesty to English as a field of study and its representatives]. In E. Kleinschmidt (Ed.). *Fremdsprachenunterricht zwischen Sprachenpolitik und Praxis* (pp. 41-49). Tübingen: Gunter Narr.

Polak, J. (2000). Bologna declaration and planned follow-up at VSB - Technical University of Ostrava. Ostrava, the Czech Republic, Technical University of Ostrava. Retrieved October 10, 2004 from www.ineer.org/Special/Bologna2000VSB.pdf

Preisler, B. (1999). Functions and forms of English in a European EFL country. In T. Bexa nd R.J. Watts (Eds.). *Standard English: The widening debate* (pp. 239-267). London: Routledge.

Rosengren, K. E. (Ed.). (1994). *Media effects and beyond. Culture, socialization and lifestyles.* London: Routledge.

Savignon, S. J. (1997). *Communicative competence: theory and classroom practice: Texts and contexts in second language learning.* New York: McGraw-Hill.

Seidlhofer, B. (2001). Closing a conceptual gap: the case for a description of English as a lingua franca. *International Journal of Applied Linguistics* 11(2), 133-158.

Sercu, L. (Ed.). (1995). Intercultural competence: A new challenge for language teachers and trainers in Europe. Volume 1: The secondary school. *Language and cultural contact,* 12. Aalborg, Denmark: Aalborg University Press.

Sercu, L. (2000). *Acquiring intercultural communicative competence from textbooks. The case of Flemish adolescent pupils learning German.* Leuven, Belgium: Leuven University Press.

Shapiro, A. L. (1999). The internet. *Foreign Policy* 115, 14-27.

Skudlik, S. (1990). *Sprachen in den Wissenschaften: Deutsch und Englisch in der internationalen Kommunikation.* Tübingen, Gunther Narr.

Signorielli, N. & Morgan, M. (Eds.). (1990). *Cultivation analysis: New directions in media effects research.* Newbury Park, CA: Sage.

Skutnabb-Kangas, T. (2000). *Linguistic genocide in education - or worldwide diversity and human rights?* Mahwah, NJ: Lawrence Erlbaum Associates.

Steinborn, P. (1992). Hörererwartungen und -reaktionen auf lokale Hörfunkprogramme [Listener expectations and reactions to local radio programs]. *Rundfunk und Fernsehen* 40(1), 75-84.

Swain, M. (1985). Communicative competence: some roles of comprehensible input and comprehensible output in its development. In S.M. Glass & C.G. Madden (Eds.). *Input in second language acquisition* (pp. 235-53). Rowley, MA: Newbury House.

Treanor, P. (2000). The language of universities. [Electronic version.] Retrieved October 22, 2003 from http://web.inter.NL.net/users/Paul.Treanor/lang.issues.html.

Trim, J. L. M. (1994). Some factors influencing national foreign language policymaking in Europe. In R.D. Lambert (Ed.). *Language planning round the world: Contexts and systematic change* (pp. 1-16). Washington, DC: National Foreign Language Center.

Truchot, C. (n.d.) English in France. Unpublished manuscript.

Truchot, C. (1990). *L'Anglais dans le monde contemporain* [English in the contemporary world]. Paris: Robert.

Truchot, C. (1997). The spread of English: from France to a more general perspective. *World Englishes* 16(1), 65-76.

Truchot, C. (2001). La langue au travail. Évolution des pratiques linguistiques des enterprises multinationals. In *Actes du symposium de l'Association Suisse de Linguistique Appliqué. Communiquer en milieu professionnel plurilingue.* Lugano, Switzerland: Université de Lugano et VALS-ASLA, pp. 73-86.

Tudor, I. (1987). Video as a means of cultural familiarization. *System* 15 (2), 203-207.

Van der Linden, E. (2001). Verengelsing [Anglicising]. Retrieved October 12, 2003 from www.angelfire.com/darkside/spiritje.

van Dinter, K. & Stappaerts, F. (2002, January 21). Nederlands in Europa [Dutch in Europe]. Radio Interview with Eric De Temmerman. *Het vrije woordt.* Retrieved October 12, 2003 from http://www.vrijzinnighumanisme.be.

Vanderplank, R. (1999). Global medium--global resource? Perspectives and paradoxes in using authentic broadcast material for teaching and learning. In C. Gnutzmann (Ed.). *Teaching and learning English as a global language: Native and non-native perspectives* (pp. 259-272). Tübingen: Stauffenburg Verlag.

Verluyten, S. P., Thiré, L. & Demarest, S. (1994). *Franse taal voor beroepsdoeleinden.* Eindrapport [French for professional purposes. Final report for the Flemish Community Education Department]. Ministerie van de Vlaamse Gemeenschap Department Onderwijs. Antwerp, Belgium: Universiteit Antwerpen.

Webster, J. (1998). The audience. *Journal of Broadcasting and Electronic Media* 42(2), 190-207.

Weltens, B., & de Bot, K. (1995). Is Dutch Just another Berber? *Language, Culture and Curriculum* 8(2), 133-140.

Wichert, L. (1997). *Radioprofile in Berlin-Brandenburg: Die privaten und zwei öffentlich-rechtliches Programm im Vergleich* [Radio profiles in Berlin-Brandenburg: A comparison of ten private and public programs]. Berlin: Vistas.

Wils, L. (1992). *Van Clovis tot Happart. De lange weg van de naties in de Lage Landen [From Clovis to Happart. The long road of the nations of the Low Countries].* Leuven-Apeldoorn, The Netherlands: Garant.

Witte, E., Craebeckx, J. & Meynen, A. (1997). *Politieke geschiedenis van België. Van 1830 tot heden* [Political history of Belgium. From 1830 to the present]. Antwerp, Belgium: Standaard Uitgeverij.

Wode, H. (1998a). Bilingualer Unterricht und bilinguale Kindergärten im Verbund [Bilingual education and bilingual kindergarten in combination]. In B.M. Marsh & A. Maljers (Eds.). *Future scenarios in content and language integrated learning* (pp. 36-47). Jyväskylä, Finland: University of Jyväskylä, Continuing Education Centre.

Wode, H. (1998b). Bilingualer Unterricht - wie geht's weiter? [Bilingual education - where to from here?]. In H.E. Piepho & A. Kubanek-German (Eds.). *"I beg to differ": Festschrift für Hans Hunfeld* (pp. 215-231). Munich: Judicium Verlag.

Appendix

Appendix A Survey questionnaire/"Can-do" scales

Appendix B Vocabulary test

Appendix C Age by research group with the mean, the standard deviation (s.d.) and the number of students from whom data are available (N)

Appendix D Student self-assessment for communicative activities concerning speaking, learning, writing and reading with the mean (m), the standard deviation (s.d.) and the number of students on which the means are based (N)

Appendix E Summary of main findings recoded on a five point scale

Appendix F Gender of students by research group in percentages of the number of students from whom data are available (N)

Appendix G Direct effects of family variables, contact and proficiency: Unstandardized estimates (maximum likelihood) for total sample (N+1570, with dummies for the distinguished groups (group Nn=reference category)

Appendix H Total effects of family variables, contact, and proficiency: Unstandardized estimates (maximum likelihood) for total sample (N=1570), with dummies for the distinguished groups (group Nn is reference category)

Appendix I Multi-sample analysis: Unstandardized estimates of total effects

Appendix A
Survey questionnaire/"Can-do" scales

Goal of the survey:

This study is about the English language, and not only that which we encounter in school but also in many other situations. We would very much like to know what opportunities you have for contact with this language, what you think about it, and if and when you use it. This isn't a language test on which you have to do really well. What we are interested in is what you personally think about each question asked.

It takes about 30 minutes to fill out the questionnaire. When a line ('....................') follows a question you are to write your answer on that line. When a number appears in parentheses ('1') you are to cross out the number that corresponds to your answer. Further instructions are on the survey. You'll find additional instructions in the questionnaire.
If you have any questions, please ask us at anytime.

1. What is your birthday? Day:................... Month:.................... 19....
2. Sex: 1. Male
                   2. Female
3. Did you have English instruction in primary school?
                   1. Yes
                   2. No
4a. Did you ever live in a country where you've had to use English to make yourself understood?
                   1. Yes
                   2. No

If no, please continue with question 4b.

If yes, name the countries in which you have used English, and give for each country how long you lived in that country.

In which country   how long
....
....
....
....

4b. Have you ever been on vacation in a country where you've had to use English to make yourself understood?
                   1. Yes
                   2. No

If no, please continue with question 5.

If yes, name the countries in which you have used English, and give for each country how often you've visited that country.

In which country   how often
....
....
....
....

5. How well do your parents and siblings know English?
For each person put an "x" through the number that seems right to you. Please answer only about family members who live with you at home.

	father	mother				siblings
	1	2	3	4		
Very good	1	1	1	1	1	1
Good	2	2	2	2	2	2
not good/not bad	3	3	3	3	3	3
bad	4	4	4	4	4	4
very bad	5	5	5	5	5	5
Doesn't know any						
English	6	6	6	6	6	6

Please give the ages of

your siblings (in years)   ....

6. Which media is there at home and which media do you personally use?

Please put an "x" in the space below each media that answers the questions below. If a particular item is not available at home or if you don't use it, just leave the space between the parentheses blank. Answer questions b and c according to your use of the media in any case, even if you don't have access to a particular item at home.

	video	CD's/cassettes	walkman computer	

a. Is this item available

at home?   ( )   ( )   (...)   (...)

b. Do you use it yourself?   ( )   ( )   (...)   (...)

c. How many hours per week

do you yourself use it?   ....

7. Do you listen to radio broadcasts in English outside of school?
                1. Yes
                2. No

If no, please continue with question 8.

If yes,
a. On which stations? ....
b. How often do you listen to such broadcasts?
      1. Less than once a month
      2. 1-3 times a month
      3. Once a week
      4. More than once a week

8. Outside of school, do you watch TV broadcasts in English? (This includes English-spoken broadcasts on non-English networks)
      1. Yes
      2. No

If no, please continue with question 9.

If yes, list the networks you watch and indicate for each network how often you watch it.

Network	less than once a month	1-3 times a month	once a week	more than once a week
....	1	2	3	4
....	1	2	3	4
....	1	2	3	4
....	1	2	3	4
....	1	2	3	4
....	1	2	3	4
....	1	2	3	4

9. About how many hours a week do you listen to music?
Please write down the total number of hours in an entire week (Radio, on CD's and other media):
............................hours

10. Do you listen to music more often with English texts or with [*Dutch/German/French/etc. selec what applies in your country, more than one if necessary in separate questions] texts?

      1. Only English
      2. Mainly English
      3. Somewhat more English
      4. About the same for each
      5. Somewhat more *
      6. Mainly *
      7. Only *

11. How important is the text to you in music?

a. For * language music
      1. Very important
      2. Rather important
      3. Less important
      4. Not at all important
a. For English language music
      1. Very important
      2. Rather important
      3. Less important

4. Not at all important
a. For music with texts in other languages than * and English
    1. Very important
    2. Rather important
    3. Less important
    4. Not at all important

12. Which opportunities do you have for contact with the English language?
Below is a list of opportunities in which one can come into contact with the English language. Make an "x" on the number that best matches your situation: "1" means "very often", "2" means "often", etc.

	very often	often	sometimes	never
a. Parents	1	2	3	4
b. Siblings	1	2	3	4
c. Friends	1	2	3	4
d. Music in the radio	1	2	3	4
e. Talking in the radio	1	2	3	4
f. TV	1	2	3	4
g. Cassettes/CDs	1	2	3	4
h. At the movies	1	2	3	4
I. Newspapers	1	2	3	4
J. Magazines	1	2	3	4
K. Books	1	2	3	4
L. Computer	1	2	3	4
M. Traveling abroad	1	2	3	4

13. Do you like the English language?
    1. Very much
    2. More like than dislike
    3. More dislike than like
    4. Not at all

14. How important is it for you to know English?
    1. Very important
    2. Rather important
    3. Less important
    4. Not at all important

15. What advantages are there for knowing English?

Below is a list of some advantages of English.
Indicate with an "x" how strongly you agree with them.

	agree completely	rather agree	rather disagree	don't agree at all
a. With English I can make myself better understood abroad	1	2	3	4
b. With English I can understand music texts better	1	2	3	4
c. With English I can manage more easily with computer and other technical equipment	1	2	3	4
d. With English I can more comfortably carry on a conversation	1	2	3	4
e. A lot of things sound better in English	1	2	3	4
f. For a lot of things there's no equivalent * expression	1	2	3	4
g. You need English for further education	1	2	3	4
h. With English I have a better chance to get a good job	1	2	3	4
i. With English I can read books in English	1	2	3	4
j. With English I can understand English TV programs without subtitles	1	2	3	4

k. What other advantages does the English language have in your opinion?

1..
2..
3..

16. How would you judge your English speaking, listening, writing and reading ability? Cross out the closest matching number

	good	rather good	rather bad	bad
a. speaking	1	2	3	4
b. listening	1	2	3	4
c. writing	1	2	3	4
d. reading	1	2	3	4

17. In the next section we are interested in your opinion about where you have acquired English.

Which portion of your English knowledge have you acquired through school instruction, which portion through the media, and which portion through other sources?

Give your approximate portions in percent. That is: write '100' if you think that you have learned all of your English in school, or write '0' if you think you haven't learned any of your English in school at all. Or whatever numbers between 0 and 100 you think is right .

Make sure the total adds up to 100%!

Through school:	...............%
Through the media:	...............%
Other sources:	...............%

100%

18. How easy would it be for you to manage - in English - the situations listed below?

Mark for each situation whether it would be easy '1', rather difficult '2', very difficult '3', or probably impossible '4' for you to do the following in English.

	easy	rather difficult	difficult	probably impossible
1. Give directions in English to foreigners/ tourists in your home town	1	2	3	4
2. Talk in English with a friend while waiting in line for a movie	1	2	3	4
3. Get information in English at a concert ticket office	1	2	3	4
4. Read a newspaper article in English about sports or music	1	2	3	4
5. Understand the lyrics of pop songs in English	1	2	3	4
6. Write a letter of complaint in English	1	2	3	4
7. Write a short essay in English about a familiar topic	1	2	3	4
8. Take a telephone message in English	1	2	3	4
9. Understand a TV interview about nature	1	2	3	4
10. Take part in English in a discussion in history class	1	2	3	4
11. Interview for a job in English	1	2	3	4
12. Translate * songs and poems into English	1	2	3	4
13. Write a poem or song in English	1	2	3	4
14. On the telephone, understand a native speaker who is talking English slowly and carefully, that is, who is deliberately adapting his language use to suit you	1	2	3	4
15. Understand news reports on the radio in English	1	2	3	4
16. In a face-to-face conversation talk about everyday subjects, for example, public transport and openings hours of shops	1	2	3	4

17. In a face-to-face conversation, understand
an English man who is speaking slowly and
carefully, that is, who is deliberately adapting
his language use to suit you   1   2   3   4
18. Introduce yourself in social situations and
use appropriate greetings and leave-taking
expressions in English   1   2   3   4
19. Understand two Englishmen when they
are talking rapidly with each other   1   2   3   4
20. Ask for directions on the street
in English   1   2   3   4
21. In a face-to-face conversation with an
Englishman who deliberately talks slowly
and carefully, indicate whether he speaks
about events in the past, the present or
the future.   1   2   3   4
22. Carry on a telephone conversation
in English with a native speaker   1   2   3   4
23. Understand an English-spoken
movie without subtitles   1   2   3   4
24. In a face-to-face conversation with
a native speaker, make inquiries in English
about everyday topics, such as train departure
times and tourist attractions   1   2   3   4
25. In a face-to-face conversation with
a native speaker, present your views
on topical issues such as the unification
of Europe or the environment   1   2   3   4
26. Explain in a shop in English
what you need   1   2   3   4
27. On the telephone, understand
a native speaker who is speaking English
as quickly and colloquially as he/she would
with another native speaker   1   2   3   4
28. Understand the English text of a
pop song on the radio that you've never heard
before   1   2   3   4
29. In a face-to-face conversation with a
native speaker, talk in English on events
in the past, present or future, using
the correct verbal forms   1   2   3   4
30. In a personal conversation with a
native speaker, understand simple English
sentences, such as "What is your name" and
"Where do you live"   1   2   3   4
31. Understand sports reports
(e.g. a soccer match) on the
radio in English   1   2   3   4
32. In a personal conversation with
a native speaker, give information about
yourself, for example, age, hobbies and education 1   2   3   4
33. In a face-to-face conversation understand
a native speaker who is speaking as quickly and

colloquially to you as (s)he would to
another Englishman.   1   2   3   4
34. Order a simple meal in a restaurant
in English   1   2   3   4

19. What is your place of birth?   ....

20 Which language(s) do you speak at home? ....

21. What is your mother's native language?...

22. What is your father's native language?..

23. What is your mother's level of education
        [*Adapt to national educational system]
        1. Primary education
        2. Secondary education
        3. Higher vocational education
        4. University education

24. What is your father's level of education
        [*Adapt to national educational system]
        1. Primary education
        2. Secondary education
        3. Higher vocational education
        4. University education

25. What is your mother's profession? ....

26. What is your father's profession? ....

27. What was your last school grade for English? ....

28 School type: ....

29. Grade level: ....

Now go on to the vocabulary test!

Vocabulary test

The last part of this questionnaire consists of a list of 120 words. Look at each word and decide if you know it. If you know it, mark the circle next to "yes", and if you don't know it, mark the circle next to "no". For words that look familiar to you, but you don't know the meaning of, mark "no". Warning: Some words in the list have been made up and aren't real words in English.

	Do you know the meaning of these words		(continued)	Do you know the meaning of these words?	
1. freeze	yes O	no O	31. make for	yes O	no O
2. employ	yes O	no O	32. take away	yes O	no O
3. moule	yes O	no O	33. plain	yes O	no O
4. control	yes O	no O	34. deliction	yes O	no O
5. damage	yes O	no O	35. climaximal	yes O	no O
6. jemmett	yes O	no O	36. troake	yes O	no O
7. initial	yes O	no O	37. parallel	yes O	no O
8. handkerchief	yes O	no O	38. alcohol	yes O	no O
9. goff	yes O	no O	39. fancett	yes O	no O
10. blind	yes O	no O	40. pruden	yes O	no O
11. content	yes O	no O	41. cart	yes O	no O
12. turn off	yes O	no O	42. trimble	yes O	no O
13. prevent	yes O	no O	43. ionopose	yes O	no O
14. solid	yes O	no O	44. dring	yes O	no O
15. lester	yes O	no O	45. quorant	yes O	no O
16. nest	yes O	no O	46. various	yes O	no O
17. expect	yes O	no O	47. simple	yes O	no O
18. put up	yes O	no O	48. baptistal	yes O	no O
19. hegedoxy	yes O	no O	49. set out	yes O	no O
20. razor	yes O	no O	50. seldom	yes O	no O
21. opinion	yes O	no O	51. practical	yes O	no O
22. strength	yes O	no O	52. glove	yes O	no O
23. washing machine	yes O	no O	53. atribus	yes O	no O
24. australian	yes O	no O	54. wintle	yes O	no O
25. annoy	yes O	no O	55. memory	yes O	no O
26. tear	yes O	no O	56. intend	yes O	no O
27. rubbish	yes O	no O	57. leave on	yes O	no O
28. capital	yes O	no O	58. district	yes O	no O
29. attard	yes O	no O	59. flash	yes O	no O
30. oligation	yes O	no O	60. break without	yes O	no O

	Do you know the meaning of these words			Do you know the meaning of these words?		
61. captivise	yes O	no O		91. sew	yes O	no O
62. arrange	yes O	no O		92. various	yes O	no O
63. silent	yes O	no O		93. print	yes O	no O
64. life	yes O	no O		94. combustable	yes O	no O
65. hold on	yes O	no O		95. crown	yes O	no O
66. steep	yes O	no O		96. industry	yes O	no O
67. dislike	yes O	no O		97. neighbour	yes O	no O
68. disaddle	yes O	no O		98. turn back	yes O	no O
69. insist	yes O	no O		99. take back	yes O	no O
70. look after	yes O	no O		100. ripe	yes O	no O
71. frequent	yes O	no O		101. sort	yes O	no O
72. perform	yes O	no O		102. method	yes O	no O
73. interisation	yes O	no O		103. catling	yes O	no O
74. pernicate	yes O	no O		104. float	yes O	no O
75. coal	yes O	no O		105. rhoden	yes O	no O
76. grain	yes O	no O		106. barite	yes O	no O
77. yallop	yes O	no O		107. popular	yes O	no O
78. punctual	yes O	no O		108. official	yes O	no O
79. favourite	yes O	no O		109. deaf	yes O	no O
80. lamble	yes O	no O		110. admit	yes O	no O
81. fancett	yes O	no O		111. australian	yes O	no O
82. whapple	yes O	no O		112. chin	yes O	no O
83. lorey	yes O	no O		113. pungid	yes O	no O
84. wealthy	yes O	no O		114. turpin	yes O	no O
85. immagical	yes O	no O		115. organise	yes O	no O
86. rapid	yes O	no O		116. tobacco	yes O	no O
87. camp	yes O	no O		117. matsell	yes O	no O
88. sparling	yes O	no O		118. duty	yes O	no O
89. blame	yes O	no O		119. secretary	yes O	no O
90. apsitis	yes O	no O		120. give under with	yes O	no O

That's all. Thank you again very much for your participation!

Appendix C
Age by research group with the mean, the standard deviation (s.d) and the
Number of students from whom data are available (N)

| Research groups | Age | | | | |
	mean	s.d.	minimum	maximum	N
Netherlands	14.30	1.43	12	18	767
Netherlands (bilingual school)	14.67	1.48	12	18	305
Flanders	16.01	.73	15	18	208
Wallonia	15.09	.52	14	16	117
Germany	15.19	.66	14	18	639
France	16.06	.96	14	18	145
Total sample	14.93	1.28	12	18	2181

Appendix D

The students' self-assessment for communicative activities concerning speaking, listening, writing and reading with the mean (m), the standard deviation (s.d.) and the number of students on which the means are based (N)

In English, you can:	Nn (N=765)		Nb (N=320)		Bd (N=197)		Bf (N=115)		G (N=627)		F (N=142)		Total sample (N=2166)	
	M	s.d.	m	s.d.	m	s.d.	m	s.d.	m	s.d.	m	s.d.	m	s.d.
give information about yourself	3.5	.6	3.9	.3	3.3	.7	3.6	.5	3.7	.6	3.4	.8	3.6	.6
order a simple meal	3.5	.6	3.9	.4	3.6	.6	3.6	.5	3.6	.7	3.0	.8	3.6	.6
ask for directions on the street	3.4	.6	3.9	.4	3.6	.6	3.4	.7	3.6	.7	2.8	.9	3.5	.7
explain in a shop what you need	3.4	.6	3.8	.4	3.4	.6	3.2	.7	3.5	.7	2.5	.8	3.4	.7
introduce yourself	3.5	.7	3.7	.5	3.2	.8	3.0	.9	3.3	.8	2.6	1.0	3.4	.8
talk with a friend	3.3	.7	3.8	.4	3.5	.6	3.0	.7	3.4	.8	2.4	.9	3.4	.8
give directions	3.2	.6	3.8	.4	3.3	.6	3.2	.5	3.5	.7	2.5	.7	3.3	.7
talk about everyday topics	2.9	.7	3.7	.5	2.8	.7	3.0	.7	3.0	.9	2.2	.9	3.0	.8
inquire about everyday topics	2.8	.8	3.6	.5	2.9	.8	3.0	.7	3.1	.8	2.3	.9	3.0	.8
sustain a telephone conversation	3.0	.7	3.6	.6	2.9	.8	2.5	.7	2.9	.8	2.0	.8	3.0	.8
present the history of your country	2.7	.8	3.6	.5	2.7	.9	2.3	.8	2.6	.8	1.7	.8	2.7	.9
talk about past, present, and future	2.6	.8	3.4	.6	2.5	.8	2.7	.7	2.6	.9	2.1	.9	2.7	.9
present your views on current issues	2.5	.8	3.3	.6	2.4	.8	2.1	.7	2.5	.8	1.7	.8	2.6	.9
Have a job interview	2.4	.8	3.1	.7	2.5	.8	2.3	.9	2.5	.8	1.7	.7	2.5	.9
understand simple sentences	3.9	.4	4.0	.3	4.0	.2	4.0	.2	3.9	.5	3.6	.8	3.9	.4
understand native speaker (adjusted)	3.6	.6	3.9	.4	3.9	.4	3.6	.6	3.5	.7	2.9	.8	3.6	.7
understand native speaker on the telephone (adjusted)	3.6	.6	3.9	.4	3.8	.4	3.6	.6	3.5	.8	2.9	.9	3.6	.7
understand past, present, future (adjusted)	3.3	.7	3.8	.4	3.5	.7	3.4	.7	3.3	.9	2.7	.9	3.3	.8
understand lyrics of pop songs	3.2	.7	3.5	.6	3.2	.7	2.6	.7	3.4	.7	2.5	.8	3.2	.8
get information about a ticket	3.1	.7	3.7	.4	3.3	.7	3.1	.8	3.1	.7	2.4	.9	3.2	.8
Take a telephone message	3.1	.8	3.7	.5	3.2	.7	2.6	.7	3.2	.8	2.1	.8	3.1	.8
understand sport reports	3.0	.8	3.4	.6	2.8	.8	2.8	.8	3.0	.8	2.2	.8	3.0	.8
understand movies without subtitles	3.1	.7	3.6	.5	3.1	.7	2.4	.7	2.7	.9	1.9	.8	2.9	.9
understand news reports on radio	3.0	.7	3.5	.6	2.7	.7	2.3	.6	2.9	.8	1.8	.8	2.9	.8
understand text of a new pop song	3.0	.7	3.3	.6	2.9	.8	2.2	.7	2.8	.9	1.9	.8	2.8	.8
understand a TV interview	2.8	.9	3.4	.6	2.8	.8	2.1	.7	2.5	.9	1.8	.8	2.7	.9
understand native speaker (normal)	2.7	.8	3.4	.6	2.8	.8	2.2	.7	2.4	.9	1.8	.7	2.6	.9
understand native speaker on the telephone (normal)	2.6	.8	3.3	.6	2.8	.8	2.1	.7	2.2	.9	1.5	.7	2.5	.9
understand two native speakers talking fast	2.5	.8	3.2	.6	2.3	.8	1.9	.6	2.4	.9	1.7	.7	2.5	.9
Read newspaper article on sports	3.2	.7	3.7	.5	3.2	.7	3.3	.7	3.3	.8	2.8	.9	3.3	.7
write a short essay	3.0	.8	3.7	.5	3.0	.7	3.2	.6	3.1	.9	2.4	.9	3.1	.8
translate songs/poems into English	2.8	.8	3.2	.6	2.7	.8	2.6	.7	3.0	.9	2.5	.8	2.9	.8
write a song/poem	2.7	.8	3.3	.7	2.7	.8	2.1	.8	2.8	1.0	2.1	.9	2.7	.9
write a letter of complaint	2.6	.8	3.2	.6	2.4	.8	2.1	.8	2.5	.8	1.6	.7	2.5	.9

Appendix E

Summary of main findings recoded on a five point scale

Variables	Nn ++	Nn +	Nn 0	Nn −	Nn −−	Nb ++	Nb +	Nb 0	Nb −	Nb −−	Bd ++	Bd +	Bd 0	Bd −	Bd −−	Bf ++	Bf +	Bf 0	Bf −	Bf −−	G ++	G +	G 0	G −	G −−	F ++	F +	F 0	F −	F −−
Highest level			×			×					×					×							×					×		
Educ. Parents																														
Eng. Proficiency Parents	×					×					×							×				×						×		
Eng. Proficiency siblings		×					×				×							×				×						×		
Contact Eng. Radio			×				×						×					×						×				×		
Contact Eng. TV	×					×					×						×					×						×		
Contact Eng. CD/Cassettes		×					×					×					×					×							×	
Contact Eng. Cinema	×					×					×						×						×					×		
Contact Eng. Computer		×				×						no data						×			×									
Listening to music	×					×					×						×				×							×		
Eng. Music mainly			×				×					×					×					×						×		
Eng. Lyrics important	×					×						×					×						×							×
Eng. TV once a week +	×					×					×					×						×						×		
Use Eng during Holidays		×				×					×						×													
Likeability English	×					×					×					×					×					×				
Importance of English	×					×					×					×					×									
Self-assessment Speaking	×					×										×						×					×			
Self-assessment Listening	×					×					×					×					×						×			
Self-assessment Writing		×				×						×				×						×					×			
Self-assessment Reading	×					×					×					×					×						×			
Can-do		×				×						×						×				×								
Vocabulary test	×					×					×							×					×				no data			

Appendix F
<u>*Gender of students by research group in percentages of the number of students*</u>
<u>*from whom data are available (N)*</u>

Research groups	boys		girls		Total	
	n	%	n	%	N	%
Netherlands	379	47.3	416	51.9	795	100.0
Netherlands (bilingual school)	160	48.8	166	50.6	326	100.0
Flanders	89	42.8	118	56.7	207	100.0
Wallonia	77	65.3	41	34.7	118	100.0
Germany	334	51.6	307	47.4	641	100.0
France	35	23.8	112	76.2	147	100.0
Total sample	1074	47.8	1160	51.6	2234	100.0

Appendix G

Direct effects of Family Variables, Contact and Proficiency:

Unstandardized estimates (maximum likelihood) for total sample (N=1570),

with dummies for the distinguished groups (group Nn=reference category)

	Family Variables					Group		
	EduPar	EngPar	EngSib	Nb	Bd	Bf	G	F
Contact								
Family/friends	--	.07***	.07***	.21***	-.10*	.13*	-.02	-.11*
Media: music/film	--	.04***	.04***	.16**	.03	-.43***	-.39***	-.84***
Media: info	--	.05***	.03***	.15**	-.10*	-.14*	.40***	-.03
Vacations	.16**	.24***	.06**	.71***	-.58***	-.12	.41***	-.26
Proficiency								
Self-assessment	.04*	.02**	.01*	.38***	-.01	-.14**	.09**	-.46***
Vocabulary test	.02***	--	--	.16***	.10***	-.10***	-.11***	-.02
Attitudes								
Estimation	--	--	--	-.18***	.18***	.63***	.04	.28***
Importance	--	--	--	.05	.36***	.37***	.30***	.11
Advantages	--	--	--	-.04	.20***	.18***	.09***	.04

	Contact				Proficiency		R^2
	FaFr	Media 1	Media 2	Vac	SA	Voc	
Contact							
Family/friends							.14
Media: music/film							.30
Media: info							.13
Vacations							.13
Proficiency							
Self-assessment	.16***	.13***	.08***	.04***			.40
Vocabulary test	.02*	.03***	--	.01***			.38
Attitudes							
Estimation	.13***	.11***	--	--	.66***	.33***	.30
Importance	.11***	.11***	--	--	.33***	--	.18
Advantages	.08***	.12***	.06**	--	.20***	--	.18

*= p<.05, **=p<.01 ***=p<.001

Appendix H
Total effects of Family Variables, Contact and Proficiency: Unstandardized estimates
(maximum likelihood) for total sample (N=1570), with dummies for the distinguished groups (group Nn is reference category)

	Family Variables			Group				
	EduPar	EngPar	EngSib	Nb	Bd	Bf	Ge	Fr
Contact								
Family/friends	--	.07***	.07***	.21***	-.10*	.13*	-.02	-.11*
Media: music/film	--	.04***	.04***	.16**	.03	-.43***	-.39***	-.84***
Media: info	--	.05***	.03***	.15**	-.10*	-.14*	.40***	-.03
Vacations	.16**	.24***	.06**	.71***	-.58***	-.12	.41***	-.26
Proficiency								
Self-assessment	.04**	.05***	.04***	.48***	-.06	-.19***	.08**	-.60***
Vocabulary test	.02***	.00***	.00***	.18***	.09***	-.11***	-.12***	-.00
Attitudes								
Estimation	.03***	.05***	.04***	.24***	.16**	.43***	.01	-.23**
Importance	.01**	.03***	.02***	.24***	.34***	.28***	.28***	-.19***
Advantages	.01**	.02***	.02***	.10*	.18***	.09	.09**	-.19***

	Contact				Proficiency		R^2
	Fa/fr	Me-mus	Me-inf	Vac	SA	Voc	
Contact							
Family/friends							.14
Media: music/film							.30
Media: info							.13
Vacations							.13
Proficiency							
Self-assessment	.16***	.13***	.08***	.04***			.40
Vocabulary test	.02*	.03***	--	.01***			.38
Attitudes							
Estimation	.24***	.21***	.05***	.03***	.66***	.33***	.30
Importance	.16***	.15***	.03***	.01***	.33***	--	.18
Advantages	.11***	.15***	.07***	.01***	.20***	--	.18

*=p<.05, **=p<.01, ***=p<.001

In the presence of English

Appendix 1
Multisample Analysis: unstandardized estimates of total effects

	Family Variables			Contact				Proficiency	
	EduPar	EngPar	EngSib	Fa/fr	Media 1	Media 2	Vac	SA	Voc
Contact									
Family/friends	--	.07***	.07***						
Media 1	--	.04***	.04***						
Media 2	--	.04***	.03***						
Vacations	.12*	.22***	.06**						
Proficiency									
Self-assessment	.04**	.05***	.04*** .01 (2,4)	.14***	.13***	.09***	.03***		
Vocabulary test	.02*** -- (6)	.00*** .00** (2,3) -- (6)	.00*** .00 (3) -- (6)	.02* -.02* (3) -- (6)	.03*** -- (6)	--	.01*** -- (6)		
Attitudes									
Estimation	.04*** .02 (2) .02*** (4) .03** (6)	.05*** .04*** (2) .03*** (4)	.04*** .02*** (2,4)	.23*** .22*** (2,3) .17*** (4)	.23*** .19*** (2) .17*** (4) .21*** (6)	.06*** .02*** (4)	.03*** .02*** (2) .01*** (4) .02*** (6)	.66*** .21*** (4)	.44*** -.69*** (2)
Importance	.01** .00 (3) .03*** (5)	.03** .01 (3) .06*** (6)	.02** (1,4) .01 (2,3) .03** (5) .06*** (6)	.13 .08 (3) .14 (5) .61*** (6)	.16*** .11*** (3) .18*** (5)	.03*** .00 (3)	.01*** .00 (3) .02*** (5)	.33*** -.03 (3)	.62*** (5)
Advantages	.01** .02** (2)	.02*** .03*** (1) .04*** (2)	.02*** .01*** (3,4)	.09*** .11*** (1) .15*** (2)	.15*** .17*** (1) .20*** (2)	.07*** .08*** (1) .10*** (2)	.00*** .01*** (1) .02*** (2)	.13*** .30*** (1) .55*** (2)	--

1=Nn, 2=Nb, 3=Bd, 4=Bf, 5=G, 6=F
*=p<.05, **=p<.01, ***=p<.001

Index

A.C.C., 20
acculturation, 5, 6
Admiraal, 56
affective factors, 12
affiliation, 8, 13
AirSpeak, 23
American popular culture, 4
Ammon, 3, 5, 27, 33, 35, 135
Anglo-American, 14, 127
Anglo-American hegemony, 132
assessment, 11, 16, 54, 55, 56, 77, 78, 88, 90, 94, 99, 110, 123, 129
attitudes, 7, 8, 9, 12, 13, 14, 16, 17, 25, 45, 46, 47, 48, 49, 52, 53, 54, 55, 62, 82, 89, 90, 91, 94, 96, 99, 101, 103, 115, 117, 120, 124, 129, 133
Austria, 28

Bachman, 11
Baetens-Beardsmore, 30
Bailey, 20
Bandura, 14
Barcelona Council, 29
BBC, 36, 37, 39, 41, 71
Beheydt, 47
Belgian, 28, 37, 41, 44, 45, 47, 63, 65, 71, 72, 79, 84, 89, 117
Belgium, 9, 16, 18, 19, 21, 23, 24, 28, 30, 32, 35, 36, 37, 39, 46, 48, 49, 57, 89, 103, 115
Berlamont, 32
Berns, 5, 7, 13, 17, 20, 115
Biersack, 23
bilingual, 10, 29, 30, 31, 40, 57, 60, 63, 64, 68, 72, 74, 79, 84, 126
bilingual schools, 57, 63, 68, 79
Bollag, 33
Bologna Declaration, 33

Bovill, 102
Britain, 11, 20, 24, 27, 41, 46, 48
Bulgaria, 1
Bulletin, 41
business and commerce, 22
Buxton, 56
Byram, 7

Calaresu, 27
Carli, 27
Carstensen, 5
causal relations, 60, 97
Cenoz, 3, 10, 19
Chomsky, 7
Clark, 56
CNN, 36, 37, 39, 71, 126
common Market, 20
communicative competence, 4, 11, 12, 27, 52, 53, 123, 129, 132
comparative approach, 132
comparative data, 62
concentric circles model, 5
contact with English, 16, 22, 36, 39, 44, 49, 52, 53, 54, 62, 65, 68, 71, 72, 80, 91, 96, 99, 104, 107, 110, 112, 114, 120, 124, 125, 126, 128, 129
CD, 104
cinema, 107, 110, 111
internet, 2
living abroad, 73, 74
music, 4, 15, 20, 35, 36, 37, 39, 40, 42, 68, 69, 71, 96, 107, 108, 110, 111, 112, 114, 117, 122, 126, 127, 128, 131
radio, 4, 22, 39, 40, 41, 44, 68, 70, 71, 104, 107, 108, 126
song lyrics, 69, 108, 111, 114, 115, 117, 122
television viewing, 9, 103

vacations, 2, 72, 73, 96, 110, 112, 114, 125, 127
content and language integrated learning (CLIL), 126
content-based language teaching, 126
contextualization, 8, 51
Coppieters 't, 24
Coppieters 't, 46
Craebeckx, 21
cross-cultural communication, 2, 51
cross-linguistic communication, 11
Crystal, 23, 48
cultivation theory, 4, 14
cultural formation, 3
cultural homogenization, 132
cultural imperialism, 14
cultural inheritance, 8
cultural orientations, 126
cultural preservationists, 14
cultural products, 36, 39, 46
cultural values, 7
Cumming, 31
Czech Republic, 34, 49

d'Haenens, 4, 39, 103
D'Haenens, 37
D'ydevalle, 9
DAAD, 34
data collection, 16
de Bens, 37
de Bot, 13, 38, 47
de Mooij, 24
de Swaan, 47
De Volkskrant, 43
Delbeke, 32
Délégation Générale à la Langue Française (DGLF, 26
Demarest, 24
Denis, 24
Denison, 5
Denmark, 9, 103

dependent variable, 91, 94, 99
descriptive findings, 62
Devreese, 32
Dickson, 30
Discovery Channel, 38
Dostal, 23
Dutch, 7, 9, 13, 18, 19, 21, 23, 24, 28, 29, 31, 32, 33, 34, 37, 38, 39, 40, 41, 43, 44, 46, 47, 48, 55, 57, 60, 63, 64, 65, 68, 69, 71, 72, 74, 79, 82, 84, 87, 90, 107, 108, 110, 111, 112, 114, 115, 117, 118, 120, 122, 128

Ellis, 8
empirical approach, 16, 124
England, 19, 48, 118
English
    African English, 11
    American English, 11, 12, 20, 25, 34
    Ghanaian English, 12
    Indian English, 12
    South Asian English, 11
    as a foreign language, 10
    as a second language, 73, 125, 132
    for international and intranational purposes, 5
English-language search engines, 40
Estonia, 49
Etiemble, 48
European Audiovisual Observatory, 36
European Central Bank, 15, 22
European Commission, 2, 4, 15, 19, 28, 43, 44, 45, 46, 127
European Union (EU), 1
Eurostat, 29
Eurovision Song Contest, 35
Eurydice, 4, 27, 28, 29, 31
Evers, 44
expanding circle, 4

family background, 53, 60
Financial Times, 41
Finland, 28, 103
Firth, 8
Fishman, 48
Flaitz, 13
Flanders, 21, 28, 29, 32, 37, 39,
    41, 46, 47, 55, 56, 68, 77, 103,
    117
Flemish, 23, 28, 39, 45, 46, 47
France, 13, 16, 18, 19, 24, 25, 26,
    28, 29, 30, 32, 33, 35, 36, 37,
    38, 39, 40, 41, 42, 44, 47, 48,
    49, 55, 57, 69, 77, 89, 103, 115,
    118, 127, 128
France Now, 42
French, 15, 18, 19, 20, 21, 23, 25,
    26, 28, 29, 30, 31, 32, 34, 37,
    39, 41, 42, 43, 44, 45, 46, 47,
    48, 55, 57, 63, 65, 68, 69, 71,
    72, 73, 78, 79, 80, 82, 84, 107,
    115, 117, 118, 127, 128

Gardner, 12
Garza, 9
Gawlitta, 25
Gerbner, 14
German, 13, 18, 19, 20, 21, 23,
    26, 27, 28, 29, 30, 31, 32, 33,
    34, 35, 36, 37, 38, 41, 42, 43,
    44, 45, 48, 49, 54, 55, 60, 63,
    65, 68, 71, 72, 74, 80, 82, 84,
    107, 108, 110, 112, 114, 115,
    117, 118, 120, 122, 128
Germany, 16, 18, 20, 21, 22, 24,
    25, 26, 28, 29, 30, 31, 33, 34,
    35, 36, 38, 40, 42, 44, 46, 47,
    48, 49, 55, 56, 57, 60, 64, 77,
    103, 108, 114, 115, 118, 122,
    128
Gerritsen, 24
Gijsbers, 24
globalism, 2

globalization, 1, 7, 51, 52, 126
glocalization, 40
Gnutzmann, 3
Goethals, 37
Graddol, 23, 40, 48
grammatical structures, 11
Greece, 18, 28
Greek, 15, 31
Grendel, 56
Guardian, 41

Hagen, 130
Halliday, 8
Hasebrink, 12, 18, 11, 12, 4, 13,
    17, 37, 38, 41, 42, 43, 101, 102,
    103, 115, 124, 142, 143, 144,
    145
Hawkins, 102
hermeneutic, 16
Herzog, 37
higher education, 22, 27, 31, 32,
    33, 34, 35, 41, 47, 48, 49, 79
Hilgendorf, 25
historical context, 17
Hofstede, 6, 7, 15
HOTBOT, 40
Huibregtse, 56
Hungarian, 1, 49
Hungary, 49
Hymes, 11

idealistic, 3
immigrant languages, 18
independent variables, 91, 99, 101
Ingleton, 23
inner circle, 5, 6
input, 4, 9, 69
intentional contact, 107
intercultural communication, 125
internal communication, 24
international communication, 6,
    14, 21, 22
International Herald Tribune, 41

international language, 6, 22, 27,
   47, 126
international schools, 30
internationalization of education,
   31
internet, 4, 22, 23, 39, 40, 52, 101,
   103, 104, 105, 127, 131
interpersonal communication, 2
interpersonal dimensions of
   language, 8
intrapersonal dimensions of
   language, 8
Irish, 1, 18
Israel, 103
Italian, 18, 29, 31, 32, 43, 44
Italy, 18, 19, 20, 26, 27, 37, 40,
   103, 128

Jagt, 38
Janssen, 38, 44
Janssen-van Dieten, 44
Japanese, 15, 26
Jessner, 3, 10, 19
Johnson, 23
Johnsson-Smaragdi, 103, 104
Jones, 56
Jorden, 56
Jöreskog, 91
journalism, 22

Kachru, 5, 8, 17
Kessels, 38
Königs, 10
Korzilium, 24
Krotz, 102, 103

Lambert, 12, 18
Lammert, 48
language
   acculturation, 5
   demographics, 17
   dubbing, 38
   environments, 117, 128
   functions, 5

   of publication, 25
   of wider communication, 10,
      11, 49
   policy, 49, 53
   purists, 14
Lantolf, 8
Latvia, 49
Latvian, 1
Le Monde, 23, 36
learning as acquisition, 8
learning *as* participation, 8
level of education, 63, 80, 84, 89,
   96
lingua franca, 6, 7, 11, 23, 27,
   123, 124, 127, 130, 131, 132
linguistic diversity, 17, 18, 19
linguistic repertoire, 12, 24
linguistic resistance, 48
LISREL analysis, 83
Lithuania, 49
Livingstone, 102
localism, 2

MacWilliam, 9
Maljers, 30
Malta, 49
Marsh, 30
Marsland, 30
Martin, 25
McArthur, 6
McConnell, 33
McDonaldization, 6
McIntyre, 12
mean scores, 44, 68, 74, 75, 77,
   78, 84, 88, 90, 94
Meara, 56
media, 2, 3, 4, 10, 13, 14, 16, 17,
   22, 25, 35, 36, 37, 38, 39, 40,
   41, 42, 44, 48, 49, 50, 52, 53,
   54, 55, 60, 62, 65, 68, 79, 80,
   83, 87, 96, 101, 102, 103, 104,
   105, 107, 108, 110, 111, 112,
   114, 117, 122, 124, 125, 126,
   127, 128, 131, 132, 133

accessibility, 39
availability, 39
contact and use, 3
environment, 101, 102, 103
products, 3
medium of instruction, 27, 30, 32, 34
Meskill, 9
Meynen, 21
Mitchell, 9
mobility, 2, 18, 31, 32, 130
monolingual schools, 57
monolingualism, 10
Morgan, 14
motivation, 8, 12, 42, 52, 53, 129, 130
instrumental, 12
integrative, 12
Motz, 33
MTV, 38
MTV Europe, 37, 126
Mueller, 9
multiculturalism, 1
multilingual, 1, 2, 3, 4, 7, 10, 27, 30, 40, 46, 130
multilingual acquisition, 10
multilingual and multicultural diversity, 3
multilingualism, 1, 11
Myles, 9

National Geographic, 37
native vs. non-native dichotomy, 6
nativization, 6
Netherlands, 9, 13, 16, 20, 23, 24, 27, 28, 29, 31, 33, 34, 35, 36, 38, 40, 43, 44, 45, 47, 48, 49, 54, 55, 57, 68, 77, 103, 108, 114, 115, 117, 118, 122, 129
Nickerson, 24

official language, 1, 18, 19, 20, 22, 26

Oreja, 14
Organization of German Music Publishers, 41
Otto, 30
Oud-de Glas, 45

Palmer, 8
pan-European public sphere, 131
Paris Free Voice Magazine, 42
Pariscope, 42
Parker, 37
Parmentier, 23
Pavakanun, 9
Peace Treaty of Versailles, 20
Pennycook, 3
personal network, 96
Phillipson, 3
phonology, 12
Piepho, 3
Pingree, 102
Plicht, 23
Poland, 49
PoliceSpeak, 23
Polish, 1, 31
Portugal, 28, 38
Portuguese, 18, 31
post-hoc testing, 83
pragmatics, 12
pragmatists, 3
Preisler, 9, 12
primary education, 20, 21, 29, 74
proficiency, 3, 6, 9, 10, 11, 12, 14, 16, 17, 23, 31, 34, 35, 43, 44, 46, 48, 49, 52, 53, 54, 55, 56, 62, 65, 77, 78, 80, 83, 90, 91, 94, 95, 96, 99, 101, 102, 104, 110, 111, 114, 115, 117, 120, 122, 123, 124, 128, 129, 130, 132, 133
English proficiency, 23, 43, 90, 91, 94, 101, 102, 111, 114, 122, 123, 128, 132
functional proficiency, 53, 55, 56

indicators, 107
language proficiency, 52, 56,
   78, 80, 115
scales, 16
pseudo-words, 56, 57
psychology, 4, 7, 12, 27, 33, 53,
   124

questionnaire, 16, 49, 54, 55, 57,
   60, 65, 73, 75, 80, 90, 103, 125

regional dialects, 18
Reynolds, 102
Romania, 1
Rosengren, 102
Ross, 37
RTBF, 39
Russia, 18, 20
Russian, 26, 31

Savignon, 11
Scandinavia, 20, 38
schemata, 9
Schils, 38
schooling, 28, 52, 126, 132
Science Citation Index, 26
SeaSpeak, 23
second language, 19, 29, 31
second language acquisition, 7
second language pedagogy, 53
secondary education, 19, 20, 28,
   29, 30
Seidlhofer, 5
Sercu, 46
Shapiro, 40
Signorielli, 14
Skinner, 13, 115
Skudlik, 27
Skutnabb-Kangas, 3
Slovenia, 49
"small" languages, 18
Smythe, 12
social background, 49, 102, 114,
   124

social learning theory, 14
social psychology, 4, 7, 12, 53,
   124
socio-economic groups, 13
sociolinguistic profile, 16, 17, 48,
   49, 51
sociolinguistics, 4, 7, 16, 51, 53,
   124
solidarity, 13
Sörbom, 91
Southern Europe, 34
Soviet Union, 21
Spain, 24, 28, 37, 40, 44, 45, 103,
   127, 128
Spanish, 18, 19, 29, 31, 32, 34,
   43, 44, 45, 127
standardized test, 56
Stanhope, 20
Stappaerts, 33
Steinborn, 41
study design and methodology, 16
Swain, 9
Sweden, 38, 44, 103
Switzerland, 22, 36, 103

technology, 2, 21, 22, 25, 41, 48,
   51, 127, 140
tertiary education, 32
third language, 19
Thiré, 24, 45
Times, 41
TOEFL, 34
Treanor, 33
Trim, 18
Troll, 23
Truchot, 3, 23, 24, 25, 35
Tudor, 9
Turkey, 18, 55, 118
Turkish, 13, 18, 19, 31, 118
TV commercials, 24

U.K., 55
U.S., 41, 46, 55

United Nations Development
Program/UNDP, 36
user status, 6

validity, 56, 97, 125
values, 14, 25
Van der Linden, 35
van Dinter, 33
van Meurs, 24
Vanderplank, 9
variety
  language varieties, 11
  national varieties, 12
  regional varieties, 11
  variety of English, 5, 25, 129
Verluyten, 24, 32, 45
vocabulary test, 16, 55, 56, 57,
  60, 77, 78, 84, 88, 94, 96, 97,
  110, 112, 114, 122

Wall Street Journal, 41
Wallonia, 21, 28, 29, 30, 32, 35,
  37, 39, 41, 46, 77
Walloon, 18, 39, 57, 117
Walters, 14
Webster, 101
Weltens, 13, 47
Wichert, 40
Wils, 21
Witte, 21
Wode, 30
workplace, 22, 23, 42, 48, 130
world Englishes paradigm, 4, 5

Yahoo, 40
young people, 1, 2, 51, 101, 114,
  124, 131, 132, 133
youth, 3

Language Policy

1. M.H. Amara and A.A. Marʻi: Language Education Policy: The Arab Minority in Israel. 2002   ISBN1-4020-0585-7

2. R.B. Kaplan and R.B. Baldauf Jr.: Language and Language-in-Education Planning in the Pacific Basin. 2002   ISBN1-4020-1062-1

3. L.A. Grenoble: Language Policy in the Soviet Union. 2003   ISBN1-4020-1298-5

4. M. Zhou (ed.) Language Policy in the People's Republic of China: Theory and Practice Since 1949. 2004   ISBN 1-4020-8038-7

5. T. Clayton: Language Choice in a Nation under Transition: English Language Spread in Cambodia. 2006   ISBN 0-387-31193-9

6. A.L. Rappa and L. Wee: Language Policy and Modernity in Southeast Asia: Malaysia, the Philippines, Singapore, and Thailand. 2006.   ISBN 1-4020-4510-7

7. M. Berns, K. de Bot, and U. Hasebrink (eds.): In The Presence of English: Media and European Youth. 2007   ISBN 0-387-36893-0

Printed in the USA